Writing for excellence

Writing for excellence

A four-stage approach to creating maximum impact in business writing

Michael Doherty

McGRAW-HILL BOOK COMPANY

London · New York · St Louis · San Francisco · Auckland
Bogotá · Caracas · Hamburg · Lisbon · Madrid · Mexico
Milan · Montreal · New Delhi · Panama · Paris · San Juan
São Paulo · Singapore · Sydney · Tokyo · Toronto

Published by
McGRAW-HILL Book Company Europe
Shoppenhangers Road, Maidenhead, Berkshire, SL6 2QL, England
Telephone 0628 23432
Fax 0628 770224

British Library Cataloguing in Publication Data

Doherty, Michael
Writing for Excellence: Four-stage Approach to Creating Maximum
Impact in Business Writing
I. Title
808

Library of Congress Cataloging-in-Publication Data

Doherty, Michael, 1944–
Writing for excellence: a four-stage approach to creating maximum
impact in business writing / Michael Doherty.
   p.   cm.
Includes bibliographical references and index.
ISBN 0–07–707654–0
1. Business writing. I. Title.
HF5718.3.D64   1992
808'.06665–dc20   92–17062 CIP

1234 M & A 95432

Typeset by Computape (Pickering) Ltd, North Yorkshire
and printed and bound in Great Britain by
M. & A. Thomson Litho, East Kilbride, Scotland

Contents

Preface

Writing for Excellence has been slowly developed during years of instruction to business personnel in many professions including legal, engineering, operations, production, sales, marketing and training. Furthermore, the research undertaken to present this book has not been confined to one culture. On the contrary, the sources and applications pertain to a global perspective.

Anyone who has to produce effective documentation appreciates one common problem: in this competitive world, image counts and image is projected in the paperwork we produce.

A successful image in written communication is essential; it requires careful construction of precise and, in many cases, persuasive information for customers, suppliers, clients, employees and management. These people, our readers, form an image of the author: the writer's communicative ability, efficiency and fluency are projected from the document and subconsciously evaluated. To achieve the image we wish to project requires (1) an appreciation of reader responses to the written word, (2) a knowledge of the aspects being assessed and (3) skill in producing the exact impact with particular readers.

If you wish to control the image you project, then *Writing for Excellence* is for you. It can be used as a self-study project or as lively and interesting course material for a report writing programme. Through a carefully structured discussion and exercise format, punctuated with models doctored from 'real-world' reports, you will be guided with avuncular care through the solutions to two central concerns:

- What are the ingredients of a success-oriented document?
- How can the image of success be projected from such a document?

Having examined the image of success in business writing (Chapter 1) we consider the constraints imposed on us by our readers, who invariably need careful analysis and diplomatic handling (Chapter 2). The essential quality factors are then identified through the analysis of a case study (Chapter 3).

Chapter 4 addresses the persuasive force factor. Gone are the days when a *mere* presentation will suffice: today people need to be addressed in a most diplomatic and sensitive way. When this has to be done in writing, the author needs certain essential skills. One of these skills is the ability to ensure fluency of rhythm and balance (Chapter 5) plus decisiveness in tone and acceptability (Chapter 6) while still projecting the formal image with a professional style (Chapter 7).

However, ensuring the appropriate words are giving the precise nuance to the controlled information is still not enough for success in writing today. Now we need to present an attractive document to make an impact (Chapter 8). To some people this may seem trifling and cosmetic: in essence it is, but in terms of creating an impression the presentation of our documents is paramount.

To assist the reader through documents we use 'road signs' or signposts, i.e. linguistic connectives. Chapter 9 examines the most important linking devices. Two documents which cause special concern for most writers are dealt with in Chapter 10. These are letter writing and reporting conversations.

In Chapter 11 all the techniques covered in the book are used to show the reader just how effective a document can be if certain commonly accepted conventions are followed.

An evaluation exercise is presented at the end of Chapter 11 to introduce some guidelines and a checklist. All exercises, including this final evaluation, have been taken from real situations and reflect realistic problems for the business writer. For all exercises a key/model is offered as an optional alternative.

Acknowledgements

I am grateful to many business executives who have allowed me to reproduce many of their documents, albeit 'doctored' for instructional purposes. Friends and colleagues who have made genuine comments on my style of instruction and my philosophy of the written word must also be acknowledged. Finally, without the continuous persistence and practical suggestions from my wife, Barbara, this book would never have reached this final stage.

1 Effective writing and the business image

Writing, in a business context, is an important element of the image we project in our working environment. For this to be positively effective three criteria need to be considered for each document we produce: the information must be effectively controlled; the language must be carefully structured; and the immediate impact must be unmistakeably appealing. To be successful on all three counts requires a systematic approach which allows you, as a writer, to think before you plan, plan before you write and revise what has been written.

Image projection

This book is about projecting a successful image. People, from fashion models to politicians, invest an extortionate amount of money in image-making. And why not? We are assessed and evaluated by the image we project through our hairstyle, clothes, shoes and even physical poise. Today, you've got to look good, bright-eyed and healthy.

In business we also project ourselves through our physical image; but priority on an appraisal list gives emphasis to the image projected in the way we communicate, both in speech and writing. It is this latter and more exacting discipline that will be focused on in this book: writing. It is more exacting because, unlike speaking, we are not 'programmed' for writing; a conscious learning process is required.

Unlike the natural and invariably spontaneous response at a meeting or during a telephone conversation, writing, in business, is considered to be the result of careful deliberation over choice of word, inflection of meaning and balance of phrase. Finally, in a business context, writing is tremendously exacting because the written word is a record, an indelible expression of that business image we project in our reports, letters and memoranda.

In the projection game it helps to *look right*; to *speak right* is a prerequisite; to *write right* confirms the indelible accomplishment of success—or failure!

Report writing is a very personal skill. There are no set rules, no natural guiding principles, no exact models of excellence. To some people report writing seems easy, natural and effortless, to others it is a painstaking, laborious and sometimes terrifying but unavoidable chore. If you belong to this latter group then this book is for you: it will make you change your mind about writing and, in turn, your approach to business paperwork. Ultimately, the book will help you to project yourself effectively in future writing assignments. This it will do by taking you through a series of carefully chosen exercises, examples, explanations and case studies, thereby allowing modification to your own personal and professional style to achieve a modern, demanding and acceptable version of the *successful image*.

In today's world of fast communication and fax machines it is becoming even more crucial to project such an image. Why then are people so reluctant to invest in this aspect of their business communication? It is probably because of an unfounded belief that their writing ability is fixed, static and beyond modification: *I am what I am and this is the way I write*. If you can change your physical image with health care and beauty treatment then you can change the image projected through written documents by applying the guidelines discussed in this book. Thousands of professional people have already done so on report writing courses, implemented throughout the world. Many business people, managers, sales directors, team leaders, supervisors, engineers, doctors and lawyers, can now attribute early promotion, or a resounding sales conference, or successful team interaction, to the image they can project on paper. Yes, your business writing is important to your overall image projection. If you want this to be a successful contributing factor then you will need to be a person who can act, a person who can fight a resistance to change, a person who believes that change is possible: something of a SOLDIER figure.

The SOLDIER image

Your first piece of action will be to determine whether your current image is the SOLDIER image. In other words, do readers of your documents see you as being:　Sensitive

Organized

Loyal

Decisive

Intelligent

Efficient and

Responsible?

Image projection exercise

If your answers to the following questions include one *No* then you will need to change your attitude to writing, you will need to improve your skill, you will need to continue through the chapters of this book so that, in future, your writing tasks become not only systematic but eventually automatic, where the outcome will always be a highly acceptable document.

Do you have the SOLDIER image?

	Yes	No
Sensitive		
Do you choose a respectful tone?	[Y]	[N]
Do you know how to achieve the correct tone?	[Y]	[N]
Organized		
Can people follow the logic of your written arguments?	[Y]	[N]
Does your information flow effortlessly through the use of meaningful and sensible connecting techniques?	[Y]	[N]
Loyal		
Can people always detect your allegiance to corporate goals?	[Y]	[N]
Do your style and format synchronize with the organizational image?	[Y]	[N]
Decisive		
Do you always write what you mean and mean what you write?	[Y]	[N]
Do your readers know that you always write what you mean and mean what you write?	[Y]	[N]
Intelligent		
Do you always use the word that gives the exact meaning?	[Y]	[N]
Are you confident that your spelling, grammar and punctuation are correct?	[Y]	[N]
Efficient		
Do you always exclude superfluous text and produce only an intelligent and intelligible minimum?	[Y]	[N]

	Yes	No
Can your reader easily access different sections of your document?	[Y]	[N]

Responsible

	Yes	No
Are all the facts in your documentation accurate and verifiable?	[Y]	[N]
Do your documents always project an image of credibility?	[Y]	[N]

If just one of your answers was *No* then the SOLDIER acronym provides a very suitable assessment screen. As a writer you are confronted with many forces (see Figure 1.1). Each one in its own way could have contributed to your circling a *No* in the preceding exercise.

Force one: the reader

None of these forces is more important, or more dominant as a controlling factor, than the reader-force. This power influences not only the content of your documents but also your tone and style of expression. You will see in subsequent chapters how this force can be skilfully handled.

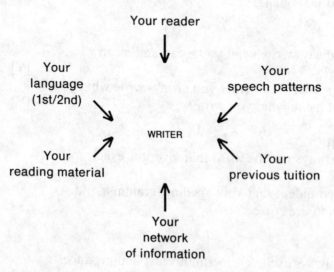

Figure 1.1   The forces against the SOLDIER image

Force two: speech patterns

A more negative force to fight is made up of the speech patterns you employ in general discussions. This informal or chatty style, referred to as *colloquial*, is still deemed tolerable and respectable in everyday conversation, even though it frequently defies the rigours of grammar and exactness. However, in your business documents, such a style is simply unacceptable. This influencing factor mars the image of many, indeed of most, business writers: therefore you will need to be vigilant, alert and in control of the techniques that will counteract this natural, yet distracting, tendency.

Force three: previous tuition

Undoubtedly, previous tuition—or lack of it—can be another adverse force. As already mentioned, there are no set rules for presenting business texts. However, over the long history of official documentation there has been an enormous and radical development in the art of presenting information. Some people engaged in the gobbledegook of the legal and insurance business may disagree. Nevertheless, the practice of business writing has changed, and is continuing to change, to meet present-day demands for quicker communication of essential information with less accent on refined and verbose discourse. Former tuition could have sown the seeds of previously acceptable habits which will require a systematic approach to uproot and eradicate.

Force four: network of information

Another force which could prevent you from projecting a successful image is really professional in essence: completeness and correctness. Your network of information needs to be constantly updated with regard to the latest facts, policies and practices of your professional circle. Clearly, a book of this nature cannot ensure your professional alertness to current specialist customs, but the systematic approach to the writing task presented here includes a tickler or two to keep you zealously sharp.

Force five: reading material

One of the more positive contributing forces in your efforts to achieve a successful image could be extant reports, i.e. documents you read and process as a part of your work. Vigilance is strongly advised. Once you have read this book you will find that documents you process as a reader may need refining. So, when you have the armoury necessary to project your particular image, diplomacy in feedback to those who report to you will be required. This will not always be necessary: some writers seem to produce effective documents with enviable consistency; from these people we learn. Samples of acceptable reports are presented in the book but, as you will begin to appreciate, a model of excellence does not exist and further editing efforts might improve even those presented.

Force six: native language

The final major force you need to contend with in your pursuit of the successful image applies if you are writing in a language other than your native tongue. The gut reactions to grammar and the assessment of a certain nuance or meaning of a word may be impaired by interference from the more versatile mother language.

If you do need to produce an important document in another language then the best advice is to have a native speaker evaluate your effort. Should the roles be reversed with a non-native English speaking colleague, then a quick processing through the guidelines and evaluation questions in the final chapter will assist you in your task.

In summary, all these forces will affect your skill as a producer of documents to different degrees and, of course, with an equally varying impact. This is as true for the bank customer requesting an overdraft facility as it is for an aircraft engineer recommending a wing-tip adjustment.

Effective document production

If you are going to deal with all these forces positively and create your documents to project the image you wish, then there are two weighty questions which must be answered.

Your first question will be:

What is an effective document?

In other words, you will need to know the criteria which decide that Document A is effective and Document B ineffective. Your next question will be:

How can I produce an effective document?

To answer these two questions satisfactorily (and for you to appreciate fully the implications for your own written work) will take up the subsequent pages of this book, with exercises, examples and feedback. However, here are the answers—used as an introductory summary—to help you begin your battles with the forces we have just reviewed.

1 What is an effective document?

There are three criteria that need to be satisfied if a document is to be judged effective:

- *The information must be controlled:* the document will contain only sufficient and necessary facts and observations, logically and cohesively sequenced;
- *The language must be controlled:* the contents will be expressed in an appropriate tone for the addressed reader, in a formal style that is grammatically accurate;
- *The presentation must be controlled:* techniques will be applied to ensure the document is attractive to the eye and clearly and consistently labelled to allow for immediate access to any part of the text.

All three criteria must be fully met: if only two are satisfied then the document will not be totally effective.

2 How can I produce an effective document?

There are four phases which provide a systematic approach to the production process: **think**, **plan**, **write**, **revise**.

Phase one: think

In phase one you will need to **think** carefully. Have a brainstorming session with yourself—ask *Why am I producing this document?* Here you need to focus on what you want the document to do: is it simply to inform, or is it going to make a recommendation? You may wish the document to be a successful request for information, a financial loan or even a change in holiday dates. Whatever your aim, it needs to be thought out clearly before you start putting pen to paper.

A further consideration will undoubtedly be your reader(s). The effect of the reader-force has already been noted. Before you even start to plan your document you will need to think about how you will achieve your identified aim with these particular readers. Will they be demanding in terms of the information they require, or interested only in the principal aim and not the supporting facts? What format usually pleases these particular readers? What chronology needs to be followed to achieve your aim with this readership? Will pictures, diagrams or tables be helpful in achieving your aim with these readers? Careful thought about *who* will actually receive the document can help you in the third consideration of this phase, namely deciding *what* information will be necessary. Indeed, the quantity and depth of information will depend on your ideas about the aim and the readership. It is far more practical and less time-consuming to sort out these aspects before writing than during the writing phase.

Phase two: plan

Once you have thought about the *why* (aim), *who* (reader) and *what* (information) you should be fully prepared to **plan** your document. You can now gather the required information and select only the data needed to achieve your specific aim with this readership. Once you have decided on the essential minimum you can now look for information which shares a similar idea or theme and group these items together, preferably under a label, e.g. Scope, Objectives, Recommendations, Problem, etc. Having decided on a suitable sequence for presenting these groupings, you will now have a skeleton of the report, in other words, a topic outline.

Phase three: write

The next phase will now be much easier: you will be able to **write** your assignment while focusing principally on the style, tone and linking techniques that will be appropriate for the paper being produced. Here considerations of fluency, word choice and sentence structure will not be hindered by issues relating to information structure. Your whole effort will now be centred on language impact by reviewing connections, eradicating ambiguities, rephrasing ideas, judging sentence balance and achieving a smooth overall information flow.

Phase four: revise

When the document has been produced you will need to **revise** to ensure that it can be understood at a first reading, i.e. it should be *clear*. The document should also be expressed intelligently and intelligibly using a minimum number of words, i.e. it should be *concise*. The techniques of presentation, style and tone should be applied throughout the entire paper, i.e. it should be *consistent*. All facts, figures and arguments should stand up to verification, i.e. the document should be *correct*. Finally, it must include only necessary and sufficient information to achieve the aim with the readers addressed, i.e. it should be *complete*.

Summary

In this first chapter you have been introduced to the image factor, which is so important in today's business world.

The most exacting projection is the image that people encounter in your paperwork. This has to be learnt: it is not natural. It must be carefully developed: it is not spontaneous. Once produced and presented, in a document addressed to your reader, the image cannot be changed: it is indelible.

There are several forces that must be controlled if you are to be seen as:

Sensitive
Organized
Loyal
Decisive
Intelligent
Efficient
Responsible

These forces are headed by reader-force and also include:
- invasion of your speech patterns
- your old habits from previous practices and tuition
- your changing and developing professional information network
- your reading of both effective and ineffective documents
- your language competency, especially if you are not working in your native tongue.

There are two questions that require answers if we are to contain the forces and produce the successful image.

First: What is an effective document?
The answer to this question requires that:
1 the information is controlled
2 the language is controlled
3 the presentation is controlled.

Second: How can I produce such a document?
Your approach to the task should go through four systematic phases:
1 Think
2 Plan
3 Write
4 Revise.

2 Common aspects of business documents

A useful way of appreciating the forces, especially the reader-force, which affect us as writers of commercial and industrial documents is to examine the influences in the production of a particular report. Of course, for a fully comprehensive assessment we would need to appreciate the working environment, the relationship between writer and reader and the network of communications from which the report emerges. Nevertheless, there are common demands our particular readers place on us which apply to all documents. These relate to the formation of the subject heading, the use of a formal written style, the application of an appropriate tone, the amount and sequence of the information input and, finally, those cosmetic touches that have a certain reader appeal.

The forces affecting a writer

Eric Pouget is a Frenchman working for a British chemical organization. He is a utilities instrument technician, working on an industrial complex where a boiler has failed to ignite on several occasions because of problems with the pilot burner system.

His initial, or operational, task was to examine the current situation and present a remedy. His second task was to produce a report for his boss, Peter Marshall, who is a maintenance engineer.

Having completed his investigations Eric produces the following document. Read it carefully because you will be asked to consider the *forces* Eric had to control as a writer in his own particular working environment.

The effectiveness of any writer depends on many issues. The most important influencing factor is without doubt the reader, in Eric's case, Peter Marshall. However, before we consider the reader-force in particular, it is probably true that other influencing forces inhibited Eric in his task of producing an effective document, i.e. invasion of speech patterns, influence from reading other documents, the quality of his information network, his lack of tuition in basic report writing practices, and probably the influence of his native French language.

To: Peter Marshall,   Date: 27.9.9_
             Maintenance Engineer

From: Eric Pouget,   Ref: ACT/136
             Utilities Instrument Technician

Subject: <u>Pilot Burner System Failure</u>

After I'd investigated the pilot burner failure during heavy rain I discovered that it was the result of two separate faults:

a. water coming into the detector terminals, and
b. water in the seal air fan ducting.

1. <u>Detector terminals</u>

   (i) A cover over the terminals would solve the problem of water entering in the detector fittings. However, that would make it difficult to get to the main burner.

  (ii) I found that 'Densotape' wrapped around the terminals was sufficient to prevent water from entering in most cases and where water did get in, it was discovered that spraying with WD40 quickly stopped the water, making it possible for the burner to be re-lit.

2. <u>Seal Air Fan Ducting</u>

   Bill Smith noticed when it was raining very heavily, a dense 'layer' of water a few feet deep was caused by the rain bouncing back up from the ground and into the seal air inlet duct which had no cover. I suggested that the ducting inlet could be moved to a dry position i.e. beneath the boiler itself. This was a good solution.

3. <u>Conclusions and Recommendations</u>

   Because of the possible high cost of a boiler shutdown, due to complete burner failure, these relatively simple and low-cost solutions must be accepted and immediately implemented.

```
Therefore it is my order that all pilot burner
terminals must be wrapped in 'Densotape' and that
the seal air fan inlet ducting be rerouted to the
underside of the boiler at once.
```

The major force affecting any writer is the identified reader. Your reader will affect you as a producer of documents in three interrelated ways: first, from an awareness of your reader's knowledge of the subject, you will determine the depth of information he or she will require for you to achieve your aim. In other words, you will need to assess what information will be necessary and what could be superfluous. Second, your reader's professional and social relationship with you will determine the style and tone. Finally, from your reader's feedback on previous documents you will appreciate the information format he or she will expect. For example, do you need to 'hit' your reader with the central or key issue and then explain yourself, or do you present a logical series of facts so that he or she can appreciate your conclusion?

Now let us assess how these considerations affected Eric's report to his boss, Peter, on the pilot burner failure.

1   Subject heading   *Yes   No*
Would Peter know what the report was about simply by
reading the subject heading 'Pilot Burner System
Failure'?   [Y]   [N]

2   Style
Does the report provide an opportunity for Eric to use
a personal style with Peter Marshall?   [Y]   [N]

3   Tone
Is the *tone* of the recommendation too strong, given
that Eric is addressing his boss?   [Y]   [N]

4   Information control
a. Would it have been easier for Peter to work down
    from the key issues, i.e. the pilot burner terminals
    need to be wrapped and the seal air fan inlet ducting
    needs to be rerouted?   [Y]   [N]
b. Do you think the maintenance engineer would require
    an explanation of 'Densotape'?   [Y]   [N]

5 Presentation techniques

Should the reader be shown a diagram of a pilot burner
system?   [Y]   [N]

Your answers to these questions should be 1 N, 2 N, 3 Y, 4a Y, 4b N,
5 N. Now let us examine the reasons.

These questions examined the principal effects on a document made
by the reader-force. As this is the prime concern of any business writer
we will need to focus on each issue independently in subsequent chapters. A precursory look at the effect each has had on Eric's 'offering'
would be worthwhile here.

Subject heading

Eric's wording of the subject heading has not prepared his reader for
what follows. For example, 'Pilot Burner System Failure' could herald,
inter alia:
* an introduction to the failure
* a modification to prevent future failure
* reasons for the failure
* effects of the failure

Eric's subject heading is not specific enough. He has not prepared his
reader to focus on the principal issue or aim of the report, which is the
proposed modifications to prevent failure during heavy rains. This
aspect of subject heading formation is very important if your search for
the successful image is to be productively rewarded. The ideal subject
heading should minimize Peter Marshall's guesswork and prepare him
with carefully synopsized details for what follows, e.g. 'Proposed Modifications to Prevent Failure of the Pilot Burner System during Heavy
Rains'.

Style

The following phrases are taken from Eric's report. Given the setting,
would you consider this style to be appropriate?

Agree   Disagree

1   Because of the possible high cost of a boiler
    shutdown, due to complete burner failure, these
    relatively simple and low-cost solutions must be
    accepted and immediately implemented.   [A]   [D]

2   After I'd investigated the pilot burner failure ... [A]   [D]

	Agree	Disagree
3 ... all pilot burner terminals must be wrapped in 'Densotape'	[A]	[D]
4 Bill Smith noticed when it was raining very heavily ...	[A]	[D]
5 I discovered that it was the result of two separate faults.	[A]	[D]

The phrases in numbers 1 and 3 may be acceptable from a stylistic point of view but, as we shall note, the tone is questionable. Numbers 2, 4 and 5 are acceptable as speech patterns but not for a document of this type. The writer's style is far too colloquial, i.e. the sentence structures show an interference from speech patterns. For example, the *After I'd* type of contraction (2) does not project the formal style, nor does the introduction of the unannounced Bill Smith (4) with his questionable opinion on the case. The emphasis on the writer (5) is a stylistic aberration from a formal written version, which should focus on the 'two separate faults' as in *Two separate faults were the cause of* ....

Another example of poor written style is the use of the word 'good' in the phrase *This was a good solution*. This is inappropriate: the word is not specific enough or in any way meaningful.

A major speech interference is what is known as *tautology*—expressing the same thing twice—accepted in speech, but without a home in business documents. For example, people may say:

I have a new hot water heater.
Can you reverse back a little?
He has a regular habit.
... entering in ...
My order ... must ...
... enforced repatriation.

The image factor is tarnished if such a practice is applied to written discourse. We shall focus later on superfluous information. Suffice at present for us to note that this invasion of patterns acceptable in speech has to be controlled by the positive application of techniques of formal written style.

Tone

If you were Eric's boss, would you accept the tone of the following phrases?

		Yes	*No*
1	... low-cost solutions must be accepted and immediately implemented.	[Y]	[N]
2	I suggest that the ducting inlet could be moved to a dry position.	[Y]	[N]
3	... it was discovered that spraying quickly ...	[Y]	[N]
4	... that the seal air fan inlet ducting be rerouted to the underside of the boiler at once.	[Y]	[N]
5	Therefore it is my order that all pilot burner terminals must be wrapped in 'Densotape'.	[Y]	[N[

Numbers 1, 4 and 5 may be thought to create an unacceptable tone for the writer–reader relationship. A boss would certainly react negatively to being told what he 'must' do and 'at once'. It is obvious that people are influenced by the tone of a document. If it is too strong the effect could be negative, rendering the writer's efforts worthless; if the tone is too weak then the impact could have a similar negative effect. The frustrating point for the writer is that the same tone might be considered acceptable and polite to one reader though downright impertinence to another!

Information control

This aspect of your report, i.e. the content and the sequence, is usually determined by the reader-feedback from previous reports. What is your assessment of the following statements?

		Agree	*Disagree*
1	In a commercial setting we should organize our information like Agatha Christie and keep the reader guessing about the key issues or aim of our document to the very end.	[A]	[D]
2	In the 'pilot burner' report the reader did not receive the main information until the end.	[A]	[D]
3	In a report of this type the aim of the document should be immediately apparent to the reader.	[A]	[D]
4	*Vis-à-vis* this report, the maintenance engineer, Peter Marshall, would not have been aware of the problem of the failure.	[A]	[D]

Your answers should be D, A, A, D.

It is not commendable to keep your reader in tension and suspense. On the contrary, to make it easy for the reader to assimilate the contents, it would be a worthwhile practice to ensure he or she knows the aim of the document very early in the reading process. This will help to minimize guesswork and form a systematic framework for you to satisfy natural reading strategies. The 'Agatha Christie' information format is therefore certainly not acceptable. The reader of the 'pilot burner' report should have received the main information at the beginning, not at the end of the document. A technique used by many writers to ensure the reader appreciates the aim of the document very early in the reading process is to allow it to be reflected in the subject heading itself. This practice should be encouraged: the effect on the reader's assimilation task is tremendously beneficial.

A final note on the information control aspect concerns common sense. It would seem obvious that the 'pilot burner' report would not have been written in a vacuous context. In all probability Peter Marshall would have been aware of this problem and the writer's recommendations. However, this does not make the report writing exercise a futile activity for Eric. There are other powers to be satisfied: for example, Peter must have a record; the maintenance file could be referred to at any time in the future; and, finally, Eric needs an official record of his operational task and proposed recommendations.

Presentation techniques

Readers like to digest the content of a report quickly. This reader-force obliges you to present your documents so that they are attractive to the eye. Certain techniques of presentation may seem cosmetic but the subconscious effect on the reader's task is a crucial element in your endeavour to create the SOLDIER image.

For example, you would need to decide whether a diagram, graph or table would ease the assimilation process. In Eric's case, a picture of a pilot burner system would be offensive and ludicrous, and therefore superfluous. However, Eric does need some advice on presentation techniques. He has been inconsistent in the use of sub-paragraph indicators. For example, first he uses *a* and *b*, then he employs Roman numerals (*i*) and (*ii*).

For headings and subheadings it is now a common practice in business documents that all major parts of speech [exceptions—prepositions, conjunctions and the indefinite and definite article] are given the upper case. Eric's subheading should therefore read: Detector, Terminals.

Perhaps, with careful advice, Eric may have written a report similar to the one that follows. Read it carefully then complete the review exercise that follows.

To: Peter Marshall,   Date: 27.9.9_
          Maintenance Engineer

From: Eric Pouget,   Ref: ACT/136
          Utilities Instrument Technician

Subject: Proposed Modifications to Prevent Failure
          of the Pilot Burner System During Heavy
          Rains

1.0 Recommendations

1.1 Wrap all pilot burner terminals in
'Densotape'.

1.2 Reroute the seal air fan inlet ducting to
the underside of the boiler.

2.0 Conclusion

2.1 The detector terminals are sometimes damp.

2.2 The seal air fan ducting lets in water
during rainfall.

3.0 Problem

Pilot burner failure has been noted on several
occasions recently. An investigation determined
that during heavy rain there was an ingress of
water into the detector terminals and also water
in the seal air fan ducting.

4.0 Discussion

4.1 Detector Terminals

It was considered initially that to cover
the terminals would solve the problem of
water entering the detector fittings. This,
it was subsequently found, would restrict
access to the main burner.

However, 'Densotape' wrapped around the
terminals was found to be sufficient to
prevent water ingress in most cases. Where
water did enter, it was discovered that
spraying with WD40 quickly repelled the
water, allowing the burner to be re-lit.

4.2 <u>Seal Air Fan Ducting</u>

It was noticed that when the rain was very
heavy, it formed a dense 'layer' of water
some two feet deep caused by the rain
bouncing from the ground. This was then
drawn into the seal air inlet duct which had
no cover. It was suggested that the ducting
inlet could be moved to a dry position, i.e.
beneath the boiler itself.

5.0 <u>Cost-Effectiveness of Solutions</u>

Because of the possible high cost of a boiler
shutdown, due to complete burner failure, it
would seem that these relatively simple and
low-cost solutions to burner failure would be
quite acceptable.

Review exercise

This exercise considers the major points covered and the revised report
given immediately above.

	Agree	*Disagree*
1 For this report the reader does not have to 'study read' to assimilate the information.	[A]	[D]
2 The style is acceptable for a document of this type.	[A]	[D]
3 There are no personal references made in the report.	[A]	[D]
4 The reader's task of assimilating the content is far easier in this report than in Eric's initial document.	[A]	[D]

	Agree	Disagree
5 A writer's objective in reporting should be to make the reader's task as simple as possible.	[A]	[D]
6 Anything which helps the reader to assimilate the information in a document should be used and anything that distracts the reader from this task should be avoided.	[A]	[D]
7 This report is written in an acceptable tone.	[A]	[D]
8 Inappropriate references to self or others can be a distractor to the reader.	[A]	[D]
9 Contractions like 'I'd' and 'we've' belong to speech not commercial writing.	[A]	[D]
10 The inclusion of information that is unnecessary for the addressed reader only has nuisance value.	[A]	[D]

11 The invasion of
- speech patterns
- the poor style of extant reports
- incorrect or out of date tuition

can hinder the production of an effective report.	[A]	[D]

12 In the revised edition of Eric's report, the writer has been

	Agree	Disagree
• *sensitive* to his reader's expectations;	[A]	[D]
• *organized* in the written expression of his ideas;	[A]	[D]
• *loyal* to company expectations of thoroughness regarding formality of style;	[A]	[D]
• *decisive* in his expression of professional recommendations;	[A]	[D]
• *intelligent* in the logical flow of ideas;	[A]	[D]
• *efficient* in the use of concise information;	[A]	[D]
• *responsible* in the confident expression of his opinions.	[A]	[D]
13 All questions, including this one, have received the 'agree' tick.	[A]	[D]

Summary

Here we have covered the major elements all writers in the business world need to appreciate. These common demands relate to:
- the function and formulation of the subject heading
- the need to apply a style that differs somewhat from acceptable speech habits and patterns
- the content and sequence of the information that is essential for our reader and aim, and finally
- those presentation techniques that make the document attractive.

3 Three quality factors

The successful document is a modest creation. It does not distract the reader's attention onto itself but discreetly allows its message to be absorbed with disciplined ease and diffident concern for its own indisputable attractiveness. It achieves this effect by a subtle yet obvious application of techniques relating to (1) the control of information, (2) the control of language and (3) the control of presentation.

A common goal for all of us who wish to write successfully in business is to create documents which forcibly yet competently accommodate reader assimilation of the data, while discreetly and deliberately precluding reader awareness of the text itself. Indeed, a successful author or playwright is generally one who can effect this ideal. It is obviously not easily achieved but you can, at least, endeavour to direct your efforts towards reaching such a target.

Many writers believe that to avoid distracting the reader from the task of assimilation is too demanding an objective. To achieve reader-friendly text is not always an easy writing task. Most effective documents—especially in a commercial context where a personal appraisal or an investment analysis or a sales pitch requires immediate, sensitive and uninhibited comprehension—are the result of exacting and taxing demands on the writer's creative and innovative powers. Writing, after all, is a consciously learned skill. From an awareness of the techniques involved to their automatic application in day to day assignments, it is a process of trial and error requiring intelligence, imagination and initiative.

Your objective when endeavouring to produce an effective report must be to make it as easy as possible for your reader to assimilate the information. If you are to succeed in this, then during the production process you must apply anything that eases the reader's task and, equally importantly, avoid anything that is distracting.

The three criteria

It is easier for us to appreciate this *use-and-avoid* technique if we consider an actual document and identify the three criteria that must be satisfied if it is to project that successful image. Since it is only possible to evaluate these criteria in a completed report you will have to direct a critical eye to a sample project before concentrating on your own

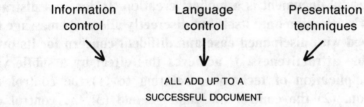

Figure 3.1 Three quality factors

efforts. But first the criteria. Let us take a report which has been addressed to you. If you have one at hand then you should use it in this exercise. The initial consideration will need to be focused on information control:

- What facts are included?
- How are they arranged or sequenced?

  If these deliberations do not cause you any great consternation, then examine the writer's language control:
- Is the style appropriate for a business text?
- Does the writer use a respectful tone?
- Are there any grammatical errors?

  Once you are satisfied that no anxiety has been occasioned by the use of incorrect style, tone or grammar, the report should undergo the final scrutiny: presentation techniques.
- Does the document look attractive?
- Are indentations correctly used?
- Is the numbering/lettering system consistent?
- Are labels (e.g. subheadings) meaningfully applied?
- Can you quickly find the information that interests you?

  Again, if you have a positive feeling on these issues then the document is effectively written: it projects a successful image.

  To illustrate all these considerations let us examine a case study. You will need to appreciate the three criteria, because the scenario is punctuated with evaluation exercises. These will test your comprehension and appreciation of the points you will need to apply if you wish to produce quality documents.

Case study

Bill Summers, the director general of Europa National Investment Corporation (ENIC), always likes short written reports on the progress of the various projects ENIC is involved in at any particular time. Presently, the government of Europa has tended to encourage investment away from Western Europe and America in favour of the subcontinent and South East Asia.

Mark Johnson, who is in charge of the Indian Project, has delegated the reporting task to Oliver Lewis, his new assistant. Mr Summers likes to be updated on events. Unknown to Oliver, Mark Johnson is one of those hypercritical chaps when it comes to report writing. Slowly, Oliver begins to appreciate this situation but it is only after several attempts and patient guidance from Mark that Oliver eventually produces what Mark considers to be an acceptable report. After all, although Oliver drafts the report, it is Mr Johnson who signs it!

This final and acceptable document is presented below. As you go through this case study you will be asked to return to it to assess the report on the three criteria: information control, language control and presentation techniques.

```
To:      Bill Summers,           Date: 18 October 19__
         Director General

From:    Mark Johnson, Director Ref: AS/1/79
         Asian Division

Subject: Progress Report One: Assessment of
         Investment Opportunities in India


1.0 Introduction

    A four-man unit has been arranged to visit New
    Delhi at the end of October 19__. I shall be
    leading this team which will include Maria Rosa,
    Peter Murphy and Oliver Lewis.


2.0 Purpose of Visit

    The delegation has been briefed to investigate
    investment opportunities. Although the team is
    not visiting New Delhi to sign any agreements,
    it will make a first-hand assessment of the
```

> liberalized investment climate in India. This
> project is a direct consequence of a major
> ministerial decision to shift emphasis on
> investments away from the West to the Eastern
> Bloc and the Third World.
>
> 3.0 <u>Arrangements</u>
>
> In order to make a meaningful assessment, the
> following arrangements have been made:
>
> 3.1 The Indian Ambassador to Brussels has
>   proceeded to New Delhi to coordinate the
>   visit.
> 3.2 A meeting has been confirmed with the Indian
>   Finance Minister, Mr V. P. Singh.
> 3.3 Leading Indian businessmen and top
>   investment, finance and banking officials
>   have been informed of the visit. Several
>   appointments have been confirmed.
>
> 4.0 <u>Follow-up Meeting</u>
>
> A fully documented report will be produced on
> completion of the visit. A meeting to discuss
> the contents of this report has been scheduled
> for 27 November 19__.

You will now be guided through a series of explanations and exercises. On completion you will realize just why Mark Johnson was satisfied that he could sign this document without any fear of a negative backlash from the director general.

Factor one: information control

The **information content** of any document will generally complement reader expectancies. If it does, assimilation is made easier and, of course, if it does not, the reverse applies.

As a reader, once you have identified the writer of a document, a writer who is part of your *own communication network*, you can guess, to a certain extent, what the content will be. This will become obvious if you consider the following scenarios.

1 You have lately written to your bank manager to ask for an overdraft. Several days later you receive an envelope addressed to you with the familiar logo and title of your bank.
  What information will you expect in this letter?
2 A relative has just gone on vacation to Spain. You receive a postcard from the Costa del Sol during the holiday period.
  What information will you expect in this document?
3 Having accepted a book that was sent to you on a trial basis, you soon receive an envelope with the logo of the bookseller on the outside. No marks for guessing the contents!

The contents of a document can be very predictable once you have identified the writer.

In the business world we know who writes to us, either by name or designation or company, and that triggers off a number of predictive operations which are usually correct. These reactions to written discourse are an essential part of our receptive operations and make it easier to assimilate information quickly. We call these operations reading strategies.

Since your readers use such techniques, you as a writer should really exploit the phenomenon. You should ask yourself: *Given the circumstances, what does my reader need to know?* Any facts additional to those presenting a succinct answer to this question will mar the effectiveness of your document in terms of information content.

Now comment on the effectiveness of the first two draft progress reports on 'Investment Opportunities in India' that Mark rejected as unacceptable.

To: Bill Summers,   Date: 18 October 19__
        Director General

From: Mark Johnson, Director   Ref: AS/1/79
        Asian Division

        Indian Visit

This is to inform you that arrangements have been made for this visit. A report will be prepared for our next meeting on this project on our return.

I will send you a copy of the report.

Of course, here there is insufficient information. Mark asked Oliver to rewrite the document, giving all necessary information. Once again, he rejected it. Why?

To: Bill Summers,   Date: 18 October 19__
          Director General

From: Mark Johnson,   Ref: AS/1/79
          Director, Asian Division

Subject: ASSESSMENT OF INVESTMENT OPPORTUNITIES IN
         INDIA: A FIRST PROGRESS REPORT

This report has been requested to keep you up to date on the progress we are making with this project.

In order to investigate investment opportunities in India, it has been decided to send a four-man team led by myself, together with Maria Rosa, Peter Murphy and my new assistant Oliver Lewis. This has now been arranged. The visit will be conducted at the end of October 19__ and the team will leave on 28th.

The principal reason for the visit is to assess and evaluate at first hand the liberalized investment climate in India. This is because the government wishes to move its focus to East Europe, Asia and especially South East Asia, where the climate for investment opportunities seems to be ideal. This is a direct consequence of a major ministerial decision to shift emphasis on investments away from the West to the Eastern Bloc and the Third World.

Letters and other communications with the Indian Embassy in Brussels, as well as high ranking financial officials in the Indian Government, have been made in preparation for our visit.
Specifically, the following arrangements have been made in order to ensure the visit is meaningful, despite the fact that no agreement will be signed.
Firstly, the Indian Ambassador to Brussels has

---

proceeded to New Delhi to coordinate the visit.
Secondly, a meeting has been confirmed with the
Indian Finance Minister, V. P. Singh. Finally,
leading Indian businessmen and top investment,
finance and banking officials have been informed of
the visit. Several appointments have been made.
These should be of interest because they have
already been confirmed.

In conclusion, as you always wish to be informed of
all matters regarding visits of this type, a fully
documented report will be produced on completion of
the visit. A meeting to discuss the contents of this
report and all matters relating to the visit has
been scheduled for 27 November 19__.

In this second attempt, Oliver has given *far too much information*. Many of the words are superfluous. This is a major weakness of numerous writers.

If you assess the information content of the acceptable report (page 23), you will note how Mark has made Oliver address the director general's expectancies. After all, Bill Summers lives in his own communication network so his reading strategies, in terms of information content, are complemented as soon as he realizes who the document is from—his assistant director of the Asian Division—and why it has been written: subject heading, 'Progress Report One: Assessment of Investment Opportunities in India'.

Let us now consider the second element of the information control criterion: **information sequence**. The ordering of the data within a document will depend on many factors. There are no overriding principles. For example, what is quite logical to one reader may not be suitable for another. The reader-force in respect to the ordering of information is very strong indeed. Some readers would prefer one way, some the complete opposite. This can be a nightmare if your boss changes too often!

Each of your writing tasks must *bend* to a mixture of controls that you will need to assess in terms of:

- the type of report, e.g. argumentative, descriptive (in terms of progress and process, etc.);
- the aim of producing the document, e.g. to make a successful proposal, recommendation, etc.

- the reader and what he or she expects in terms of chronology, e.g. recommendation first or justification first.

You will find that, except in the case of the report which is so long that it requires a table of contents, most writers order their ideas in line with the logical argumentative sequence of thought processes:

Because 'A' was the case,	*We have been studying your account recently and find that you have exceeded your overdraft limit.*
and 'A' + n is now the case,	*We are quite prepared to make arrangements to suit any reasonable new demand you may have.*
'A' can be modified accordingly.	*Therefore your limit can be adjusted subject to notification and agreement with regard to your current demands.*

However, this is not always the most suitable sequence for presentation.

Compare the different sequences in the following documents and you should appreciate how the bank manager has allowed herself to *bend* to the mixture of controls: the type of report, her aim and reader expectancy. Would you consider the different sequences to be *suitable* in each case?

To: Ms Successful	*To:* Mr Student (a potential Mr Successful)
Account No: 08–246	Account No: 08–3674
We would like to inform you that, subject to agreeable terms and conditions, we can increase your overdraft facility to meet your new demands.	A recent study of your account shows that you have exceeded your overdraft limit.
Indeed, we are quite prepared to make arrangements to suit any reasonable new demand you may have.	We are quite prepared to make arrangements to suit any reasonable new demand you may have.
A recent review of this account has revealed that you now require	Therefore, your limit can be adjusted subject to notification and agreement with regard to these current demands.

an adjustment to the current arrangement.

We therefore look forward to hearing from you shortly.

We look forward to hearing from you shortly.

You were asked to assess whether the sequences in the above texts were *suitable*, not *logical*. In each text the information is the same; the sequence is different but *suitable* for the recipient. Now assess the following two documents in a similar manner.

First comment on the suitability of the sequence in the following extract from a report written to Steve Jones, a field engineer working for a large oil servicing company who was anxiously waiting for a recommendation from his corrosion engineer, Paul Watts.

To: Steve Jones, Manager, Engineering

From: Paul Watts, Corrosion Engineer

Date: November 8, 19__

Subject: CP—1 Separator — Long Term Protection

Recommendations

1. Clean out all loose solids from the separator.
2. Dry the separators out completely. Ensure any
   dead legs between the separators and isolation
   valves are also emptied.
3. Close up all the manways and blind off any open
   flanges to ensure no air can enter the vessel.

Discussion

It is impractical to remove the internals of the
separators. The separators will therefore still
contain some scale solids plated out on these
internals. These scales are a mixture of iron
sulphides and iron oxides.

There are a number of ways of protecting the vessel
from corrosion. For corrosion to occur water and
oxygen and/or water and bacteria must be present in
the vessel. The pros and cons of the various methods
are as follows:

Here Paul thought that no introduction was necessary. He decided to sequence from important information to least important. For Steve Jones the recommendations are vital and Paul has 'hit' the reader with these from the outset.

Now study the sequence of information in the second report. You will be asked to make a comparative assessment of this document with that of the corrosion engineer, Paul Watts. Note both writers work for the same oil servicing company.

To: Bob Stout, Safety Superintendent

From: Fred Humphries, Operations Supervisor

Date: 1.1.9_

Ref: MID/1/92

Subject: <u>Incident During An Acid Transferring</u>
         <u>Operation</u>

On 28 December 19_ at approximately 0730 hours, a minor spill occurred when a tanker truck was transferring acid to a boat using a compressor to accelerate delivery.

1.0 <u>Causes of the Incident</u>

    1.1 In the vessel acid tank there was
        considerable pressure.
    1.2 Air from the vessel's tank back-flowed
        through the tanker when the compressor was
        shut down.
    1.3 Acid was pumped against a closed valve.
    1.4 The valve was not placed on the acid tanker.

2.0 <u>Effects of the Incident</u>

    2.1 Acid was forced through the tanker hatch.
    2.2 About five gallons were spilt.
    2.3 Several personnel complained of eye
        irritation.

3.0 <u>Crew Reaction</u>

    There was a quick reaction by using the standby
    water hose to wash the jetty.

4.0 Recommendations

4.1 A valve should be placed on the acid tanker.
4.2 During this operation the crew should have
   eye protection.
4.3 A course in transferring chemicals ought to
   be organized.

Now that you have carefully studied the information sequence of both reports, indicate your opinion of the following comparative statements.

To: Steve Jones,
   Manager, Engineering
From: Paul Watts,
   Corrosion Engineer

To: Bob Stout,
   Safety Suptd.
From: Fred Humphries,
   Operations
   Supervisor

1.   Steve Jones was waiting for
   Paul's recommendations.

   [T]   [F]

1.   Bob Stout was waiting for
   Fred's recommendations.

   [T]   [F]

2.   Steve does not have to read
   the entire report to
   appreciate Paul's
   recommendations.

   [T]   [F]

2.   Bob does not have to read
   the entire report to
   appreciate Fred's
   recommendations.

   [T]   [F]

3.   Paul first had to give Steve
   the reasons for his
   recommendations so that his
   reader would fully
   appreciate their significance.

   [T]   [F]

3.   Fred first had to give Bob
   the reasons for his
   recommendations so that his
   reader would fully
   appreciate their significance.

   [T]   [F]

4.   Steve was not interested in
   supporting information.
   What he required in this
   instance was the professional
   opinions of the corrosion
   engineer.

   [T]   [F]

4.   Bob was not interested in
   supporting information.
   What he required in this
   instance was the professional
   opinions of the operations
   supervisor.

   [T]   [F]

5.	Because Paul placed his recommendations first, his sequencing of information is correct.	5.	Because Bob placed his recommendations last, his sequencing of information is correct.

[T]   [F]   [T]   [F]

Correct answers   *Correct answers*
1T, 2T, 3F, 4T, 5T   1F, 2F, 3T, 4F, 5T

With regard to the sequence of information, it is important to note that there is not one overriding order that is applicable to all reports. What was true of Paul's report in the first four statements above was not so for Fred's report: yet both can be deemed *suitable* in terms of sequence, so they both get a [T] in statement five.

If you now go back to the report on page 23 and assess for yourself the information sequence, you will note that the director general can easily follow the logical sequence of the document:

First   – an explanation of the visit
Second – reasons for the delegation
Third   – arrangements to date, and
Fourth – date of follow-up meeting.

Any other order of these four topics would not synchronize with the reader's expectancy strategies.

Factor two: language control

Now that we have accounted for Mark Johnson's acceptance of Oliver's information control—content and sequence—let us examine the language control aspects of **style** and **tone**.

Each of these aspects forms the core of two subsequent chapters but here you will, once again, be asked to assess Oliver's efforts in these areas by considering two sets of exercises relating to each topic.

Style

If the elements of formal written style are not properly applied, your reader's task can be very difficult indeed. Consider the written style of the following short inter-office communication. Of the two versions, which do you prefer, A or B?

Text A

```
To:        Colin Shaw
           Manager, Office Operations

From:      Garth White
           Senior Mechanical Engineer

Date:      October 9, 19__

Subject:   LBC Entire Print Facility
           Request to Surplus as Scrap
```

We'll be decommissioning and removing the LBC Entire Print Facility in early 19__. We can then install a smaller but more powerful unit at the same place.

I'd like you to give the go-ahead to allow the existing facility to be considered as scrap. We'll then be able to break it up into small pieces if removal as one unit is going to cost us too much.

We had asked for ten local computer companies to bid for the left-over facility for taking it away as a whole or in parts but by the time the closing date arrived we hadn't got any bid.

I now think this facility is worth nothing.

Text B

```
To:        Colin Shaw
           Manager, Office Operations

From:      Garth White
           Senior Mechanical Engineer

Date:      October 9, 19__

Subject:   LBC Entire Print Facility
           Request to Surplus as Scrap
```

The LBC Entire Print Facility will be decommissioned and removed in early 19__ to permit installation of a smaller but more powerful unit at the same location.

> It is requested that approval be given to allow this
> existing facility to be surplused in place as scrap.
> This will permit breakdown of the facility into
> small components should removal as one unit prove to
> be uneconomical.
>
> In order to identify any residual value of the
> facility, bids were solicited for disposal as either
> a facility or as component parts. Ten local computer
> companies had been invited to bid but on the closing
> date no bids had been received.
>
> It is therefore concluded that the facility has
> value only as scrap.

If you chose version **B** then you have selected the style that is commonly accepted as correct in commercial writing. The style used in version A is far too personal, conversational and informal. Commercial documentation tends to be impersonal and formal, focusing the reader's attention on the topic under consideration rather than on the writer. Personal references are kept to a minimum, contractions are avoided and colloquial words and phrases, acceptable in oral discourse, are deemed absolutely inappropriate. On reviewing our report on page 23 you will see that Oliver has indeed acknowledged these practices, thereby meriting Mark's approval.

Tone

You will probably write to different people using a different style—or rather a different **tone**. This aspect of your report will depend either on:
- the relationship you have with your reader
     and/or
- the clarity or certainty of the issues you wish to express.
    Compare the following pairs of sentences and note the difference in tone.

1.a. Get that report on my desk by 9 o'clock tomorrow.
  b. Do you think you could have that report ready by 9 a.m. tomorrow?

2.a. The section could be highly corroded so we may have to consider replacing it.
  b. The section is highly corroded so we must replace it.

3.a. The yen could begin falling against the dollar at any time.
  b. The yen will begin falling against the dollar next month.

4.a. We may have to consider an entire shutdown.
  b. We shall have to consider an entire shutdown.

5.a. Employees ought to wear their ID cards at work.
  b. Employees must wear their ID cards at work.

Yes, for each pair where one sentence seemed hard, direct and authoritative, the other seemed soft, tentative and unsure. Sometimes you will need to project one type of impact on your reader, sometimes the other.

Deciding on the tone you will use in your documents is considered in detail in Chapter 6. Here it is necessary for you to appreciate that there are different tones used in different circumstances and each requires different language techniques. This topic is very important, for an inappropriate tone can make an otherwise acceptable document *entirely* unacceptable.

Oliver has obviously 'tuned' his report into an acceptable tone otherwise Mark would have insisted on another rewrite. If you review the final version, you should appreciate the 'feel' Oliver has intentionally created in terms of appropriate impact, given the writer–reader relationship and the subject matter of the document. Even one small lapse or unsuitable inflection could have had a disastrous effect not only on the effectiveness of the document but on the writer–reader relationship. Where this relationship is a salesman/prospect or employee/employer or bank manager/customer, the aberration could be very expensive. The necessity of achieving the exact climate is therefore very important indeed for the successful writer. The appropriate climate is produced by language devices which create specific tones.

The final language aspect of grammar was deemed acceptable by Mark Johnson. So, Oliver has scored highly on information control—content and sequence—and language control—style, tone and grammar. Now we are ready to assess the third criterion of an effective written document, which is the presentation techniques applied.

Factor three: presentation techniques

If techniques of presentation are not applied to create an attractive report and make it easy for your reader to find specific information, then the document will not be effective. Such a document is presented below for a quick evaluation.

This report deals with various methods of clearing
oil spills at sea for the purpose of recommending
the most effective method to be used by this
Company. Attempts have been made to burn oil.
Although wicking materials have been used to sustain
burning on the sea, they have not been completely
successful. It is not possible to burn oil on the
beach without special equipment. Burning may be
useful as a tool for dealing with fresh oil that
comes ashore or in sheltered waters close to the
shore. It is not an effective method for disposing
of spilt oil. Sinking agents are used to sink oil by
distributing a fine powder over the oil to increase
its density. This is a difficult operation and it
has been found that the sunken oil reaches the sea
bed in a form that might well contaminate fishing
gear and be detrimental to bottom flora and fauna.
Nevertheless, the method can be improved by treating
sand with amine to make it oleophilic, and applying
it as a sand/water slurry. Both methods are
effective, but have disadvantages, and therefore
should be used in emergency only. Booms may be used
to prevent the spread of oil over a wide area in the
open sea or in calm water. There are three methods
of using the booms: first towed by a suitable tug,
second moored in shallow water and third free
floating. However, oil escapes from underneath booms.
Moreover, they cannot be used in rough conditions.
Although booms have proved useful in containing oil
for recovery, they are not 100% effective.
Dispersants are chemicals used for breaking up spilt
oil at sea and these have been found to be the most
satisfactory method of attack. Achieving the best
results with dispersant chemicals depends upon two
factors: first, the distribution of the appropriate
amount of the chemical over the floating oil, and
secondly, the mixing or agitation of the treated oil
with the upper layer of the sea. Equipment which has
proved highly successful in performing the mixing
requirement is available and can be fitted to any

```
tug. Despite the huge quantity used to break up the
floating oil, it causes negligible harm to marine
life. An indepth study revealed that using
dispersants is the most effective method. Dispersant
chemicals should be introduced to the department and
adequate quantity stored in case of oil spills in
this area. One of the most efficient and least toxic
of this new family of dispersants is produced under
the trade name BP 1100X, and it is recommended that
an order for this should be placed with the
manufacturers immediately.
```

It is obvious that this type of presentation is going to make it very difficult for the reader to assimilate quickly; it is unattractive and difficult to access for specific information. The only reason for this negative assessment is that the writer has not applied presentation techniques:

Who is the document addressed to?	We don't know
Is there a date?	No
Where is the subject heading?	Non-existent
Could the writer have used space between the various topics?	Yes
Could these topics have received a label or subheading?	Yes
Would a numbering system have made the reader's task easier?	Yes

Does the report score highly on:
- Information control?
- Language control?

It is certainly possible (see Chapter 8).

A final assessment of Oliver's efforts will reveal that he has consistently used acceptable presentation techniques which certainly help the reader's task of assimilation. They also help to achieve that elusive but clever effect of concentrating reader effort on the reading task and not on the report itself.

Review exercise

Identify two aspects for each of the three criteria you have examined in this chapter where the following short report fails to support the arguments you have been studying.

The head of the training section in one of the banks in Europa was asked to evaluate the proposition that no one from the bank should be sent abroad on training courses in future. On completion of his 'operational task' he decided to write a report recommending that the Europa Bankers Training Centre should be approached to implement these courses.

To: VP, Personnel   REF: FGS/12

From: Head of Training   DATE: 6.10.9__

Subject: Provision by EBTC for Future Training
          Courses

1. Terms of Reference

   During last month's management meeting, it was
   proposed that all future training courses should
   be held at the Europa Bankers Training Centre
   (EBTC), and that employees should no longer be
   sent on external courses. I've been asked to
   review the advantages and disadvantages of this
   proposal, and to present my recommendations for
   the bank by 10.10.9_.

2. Advantages of the Proposal

   a. Where a group of employees is concerned, it is
      considerably cheaper to hold an EBTC course
      than to send a large number of individuals on
      external courses.
   b. Professionals and consultants at EBTC can be
      asked to make a course specific to our bank's
      needs.
   c. In case of a true emergency, employees remain
      in Europa and can easily be recalled.

3. Disadvantages of the Proposal

   a. In certain cases a particular specialist
      course is needed by only one or two employees
      per year. It is then more effective to send
      employees to an external course than to

arrange for EBTC to set up the programme for us in Europa.
b. Past experience has shown that departments frequently call employees away from EBTC courses unnecessarily. This can greatly reduce the effectiveness of the course for these personnel.
c. Many employees report that they receive great professional benefit from contact with other participants on external courses.
d. Bank personnel will miss an opportunity to enjoy themselves abroad.

4. Recommendations

(a) When a substantial number of employees require the same course, then EBTC programmes should be held.
(b) Employees must still be sent on external courses when it is more effective to do so.

5. Conclusions

Although there are obvious advantages to EBTC programmes, a proposal to completely reject the use of external courses would seem to have as many disadvantages, in particular the cost of providing highly specialist courses for a small number of staff.

Model answers

Information control

1. The recommendations should be placed after the conclusions.
2. Point 3d should not have been included.

Language control

1. The style of the sentence, *I've been asked to ...* in the Terms of Reference is far too personal.
2. In 4b the word *must* creates a hard tone that is inappropriate for addressing the vice-president of personnel.

Presentation techniques

1. Conclusions should not be indented in section 5.
2. There is inconsistency in bracketing or not bracketing the letters.

Summary

In this chapter you have seen how all three aspects of your documents must be effective if you are to present information that is easy for your readers to assimilate. The ultimate assessors of your documents will be your readers, who will quite subconsciously assess effectiveness. A truly important fact is that they will only become conscious of this critical function if they encounter an aberration from the norm: if their expectancies of the data, the language and the presentation are not complemented. It is your task as a writer to see that you have projected the quality factors of that successful image, thereby keeping the readers' 'natural' critical awareness of defects in abeyance.

4 Being reader friendly

One of the major reasons for writing in a business context is to persuade readers to accept new ideas, propositions and policies that can accommodate the perennial changes in the circumstances which produce the throb of the modern commercial network. Positive impact, quick assimilation, and easy access to your intentions are reader priorities.

The persuasive document is by definition an argumentative text. When you need to write such a paper you will follow the productive procedure of report writing in general. There is first the *operational task:* the scheduling, monitoring or evaluating, followed by the *reporting task* where results are recorded. It is necessary to realize this distinction of tasks to avoid confusion, for both tasks have an **aim**. Our considerations are with the successful accomplishment of the aim of the reporting task, not with your professional or operational activity. The following comparisons should help in clarifying this distinction.

Operational task	*Writing task*
Replacing a new flow valve	Report on operations carried out
Deciding on your holiday destination	A letter to your travel agent
Comparison of projected sales with projected cost of sales	Cash flow report
Check on the operations of a machine	Maintenance report
Review of current overtime practices	Recommendation to introduce a flexitime system
Meeting to discuss loan facilities for a bank	Minutes of a meeting or call report
Evaluation of the present photocopier together with a study of photocopiers on the market	Proposal to purchase a new photocopier

Operational task

Meeting during which a new policy regarding the filing system was confirmed to be operational as of the first of the following month

Writing task

Informative document to those affected by the new policy

In terms of image projection, the tasks listed in the second column are not just as important as the operational task but more important. This, after all, is ultimately where the SOLDIER image is produced.

Selling the aim

The aims of reporting tasks could be to inform, order, request, recommend, demand, suggest, advise, propose, instruct, persuade, etc. For most of us reporting generally means persuading: our reports are of an argumentative nature, expressing a medical, legal, financial, administrative—in a word—a professional opinion about a patient, client, event, situation, action, schedule, etc. This is why we were originally employed: to perform our operational tasks and report on them. You are therefore selling an idea. Now, as any effective negotiator will tell you, you never *sell* anybody anything: the trick is to create an environment where the other person will, of necessity, buy.

This underlying psychological phenomenon also applies to your reports, where you are *selling* your professional opinion. So, you have in this type of report an added complexity: not only must you make the report easily comprehensible but you must persuade your reader to accept whatever you recommend, propose, or even demand. The most effective way of doing this is to let your reader know exactly what it is you are aiming for, before supporting your claim with clever, cogent and convincing arguments. You will need to do this so that your reader will appreciate your aim *quickly*, *clearly* and *without too much effort*. In other words, you must 'hit' the reader with your aim *early* in the document, with terms that *reflect your aim*, and in a *minimum number of words* i.e. in the subject heading. So your **aim** should be reflected in the subject heading.

Formulating the subject heading

When you consider the subject headings that follow, indicate their usefulness to readers in terms of preparing them for an argumentative written discourse. The exercise may seem obvious and simple but the point it conveys is important and seldom appreciated.

		Not useful to the reader	Useful to the reader
1	Holiday Vacations	[ ]	[ ]
2	Summer Schedule of Holiday Vacations	[ ]	[ ]
3	Yoshiki Umezawa	[ ]	[ ]
4	The Promotion of Yoshiki Umezawa to Chief Accounts Clerk	[ ]	[ ]
5	Account L61258	[ ]	[ ]
6	Proposed Closing of Account L61258	[ ]	[ ]
7	Training Schedule	[ ]	[ ]
8	Suggested Training Schedule for Mrs Rosa Beaumont	[ ]	[ ]
9	Temperature Controllers	[ ]	[ ]
10	Proposed Replacement of Temperature Controllers	[ ]	[ ]

If you have ticked the first column for all the odd numbers and the second for the even numbers then you obviously appreciate how a subject heading ought to be formed.

Does the following subject heading reflect the aim of the document?

```
To:      All Section Heads       Date: 28.10.9_

From:    Head of Operations Dept.  Ref:  WP/862

Subject: Wordstar


The above mentioned word processing software was
discussed lately as a possible package for use
throughout the entire bank. This has now been
considered and it has been decided that as from
1 December 19__ all computer operators will be using
this software.
```

Now compare this with the subject heading of the following document.

To: All Section Heads   Date: 28.10.9_

From: Head of Operations Dept.   Ref: WP/862

Subject: Adoption of 'Wordstar' as Standard Word
          Processing Package for the Bank

As from 1 December 19_ all computer operators will
be using this software.

Now assess the following statements.

		True	False
1	The aim of the writer is expressed in the subject heading of the first document.	[T]	[F]
2	The aim of the writer is expressed in the subject heading of the second document.	[T]	[F]
3	On reading the subject heading of the first memo the reader is fully prepared for the information in the document.	[T]	[F]
4	On reading the subject heading of the second memo the reader is fully prepared for the information in the document.	[T]	[F]

Answers   1F, 2T, 3F, 4T

Identify the aim of the following memo, which was written by a credit relations officer of the Europa National Bank to his supervisor, then propose a suitable subject heading for the text.

The account of Europa Building Company, No. 08 9046
8154, has been reviewed again because sufficient
funds were not provided to cover three cheques
issued since our last communication with the
Manager, Mr Fernando, about this practice.

Mr Fernando has failed to reply to the numerous
written warnings we have made about this matter.

> Furthermore, he has refused to meet me or to speak
> to me over the telephone.
>
> It is therefore recommended that this account should
> be closed until such time as representation is made
> to the Bank to review the services offered to EBC.

If the credit relations officer is to produce an effective document by letting the reader know his aim or purpose in sending this memo then the quickest, clearest and easiest way is to let it be known in the subject heading. His aim is to recommend that Account EBC No. 08 9046 8154 should be temporarily closed, so his subject heading ought to reflect this:

Proposed Closure of Account EBC No. 08 9046 8154

Now test your grasp of this relationship by forming appropriate subject headings for the following aims:

1 To warn people who are not using their allocated parking slots.
2 To order the immediate use of ID cards.
3 To recommend the installation of a laserjet printer in all departments.
4 To suggest additional training for all new graduate employees.
5 To notify employees of the immediate introduction of the new personnel medical scheme.

Now compare your version with the following. You may not have exactly the same but there should be a close resemblance.

1 Failure to use Allocated Parking Slots.
2 The Immediate Use of ID Cards.
3 The Installation of Laserjet Printers in All Departments.
4 Additional Training for All New Graduate Employees.
5 Immediate Introduction of the New Personnel Medical Scheme.

Working to the conclusion

Now that you have identified the relationship between your aim and the subject heading, let us go one step further. When you are expressing a professional opinion your aim is obviously to argue towards a conclusion that will earn your reader's approval. In its simplest form the argument is first introduced:

e.g.   Many people in this company smoke.

It is then developed by adding supporting idea number one:

e.g.   Smoking is unhealthy even for those who do not partake in the habit.

Then supporting idea number two:

e.g.   If smoking were prohibited everyone would be able to work in a
        healthy environment.

It is then concluded:

e.g.   Smoking should be totally prohibited in this organization.

You will notice that it is the conclusion which is the writer's main issue, his aim in putting pen to paper. In this simple example the writer's aim was to recommend the prohibition of smoking in the organization.

It would seem that your aim is not only mirrored in the subject heading but emphasized in the conclusion. There seems to be a definite relationship between the Conclusion, Aim and Subject Heading in documents of an argumentative nature, where a writer presents or rather *sells* a professional opinion.

Ray Taylor, the operations manager of the computer division of a large manufacturing firm, may not have been aware of this phenomenon or else his subject heading would have been more helpful to Frank Green's assimilation task.

```
To:      F. Green, Maintenance Dept.
From:    R. Taylor, Manager, Computer Division
Date:    3 March 19__
Subject: Computer Room

Problems are beginning to occur in the following
areas.

Dust and Dirt Contamination
The area around the ceiling ducts is extremely dirty
and large amounts of dust particles are visible on
the computer surfaces, even though cleaning is
performed daily. This is unacceptable as IBM require
that the computer room be as dust free as possible.
```

Cold Air Supply

The ducts are wired fully open, yet the cold air
supply is not sufficient to cool the room unless the
backup air conditioning unit is running.

Thermostat Control

There is no separate thermostat control for the
computer room and therefore we have no control over
fluctuating temperatures.

In addition to these problems, we have changed a
number of machines in the computer room recently and
feel that a review of the air conditioning
requirements is essential. Details of heat generated
by all machines is available on request.

Please attend to this matter as soon as possible.

R. Taylor

Now assess the following statements.

		True	False
1	The writer's aim is reflected in the subject heading.	[T]	[F]
2	The writer's aim is to recommend a new computer room.	[T]	[F]
3	The writer's aim is reflected in the concluding paragraph of the document.	[T]	[F]
4	The writer's aim is reflected in the introductory paragraph of the document.	[T]	[F]
5	The writer's Conclusion, Aim and Subject Heading are all the same.	[T]	[F]

Answers 1F, 2F, 3T, 4F, 5F

Now if the subject heading had been:

Request for a Review of the Computer Room Air Conditioning System

then the writer's aim would have been reflected in the subject heading and the reader would have known it immediately, making his task easier. Furthermore, statement 5 above would have been *true*.

In either event, statement number 4 would be *false*, and for the task of selling your opinion this is ideal. You do not have to waste the introductory paragraph of your argumentative report by letting the reader know what it is you want. He already knows: it is succinctly expressed in your subject heading.

This now releases your creative and persuasive skills to use this section, the introduction, as a base, a foundation for your arguments. As Ray Taylor states:

> *Problems are beginning to occur in the following areas.*

Frank Green, responsible for ensuring a safe and steady ship, is immediately alerted to the situation. Ray is now able to persuade Frank with a series of arguments that *what he wants* must be approved. The final issue courteously, but effectively, concludes his text: a master touch to the successful image projection.

> *Please attend to this matter as soon as possible.*

In the following exercise you will be asked to evaluate this effective and persuasive approach to report writing—when the author needs to *sell* his or her professional opinion. The assessment will concern only the three aspects discussed, namely the writer's

> Conclusion
> Aim
> Subject Heading

Here are two different scenarios.

Case one

The senior development engineer in an oil-producing company has been warned that the computerized daily production files for all the producing wells are already heavily overloaded. One of the development programmers has investigated the frequency of access by the production department (operational task) and has proposed a solution presented in the document below (report writing task).

To: Senior Development   Date: 14.12.9_
         Engineer

From: Development Programmer   Ref: DE/28/4/2

Subject: Proposed Modification to Daily
         Production File

The space on this file has recently been increased
to accommodate the constant daily build-up. However,
the HQ System Engineer has advised that a reduction
of this space must be imminent.

As the file is continuously being accessed for data,
both from start-up point and from recent entries, it
is proposed to divide the file into:

a. Stored data, 15.12.82 to 31.12.85.
b. Current data, 01.01.86 to present.

The former data is less frequently accessed and
would only be available 'on file' with the current
file once every six months for a period not
exceeding 14 days. At other times it would be stored
on tape.

This solution would both free space available on the
current file and satisfy the needs of those
requiring full history data on a less frequent
basis. However, such a solution would need to
synchronize with current interface programs of users
of the current practice.

It is proposed that this modification is approved
before 31.12.9_.

Now assess the following statements.

		True	False
1	The writer's aim is reflected in the subject heading.	[T]	[F]
2	The writer's aim is to recommend daily access to files.	[T]	[F]

		True	*False*
3	The writer's aim is reflected in the concluding paragraph of the document.	[T]	[F]
4	The writer's aim is reflected in the introductory paragraph of the document.	[T]	[F]
5	The writer's **Conclusion, Aim** and **Subject Heading** are all the same.	[T]	[F]

Answers 1T, 2F, 3T, 4F, 5T

Case two

The day after two tellers had had an argument over a problem to do with procedures at the counter, the branch manager received a telephone call from the Central Bank which was investigating the matter. Since the affair had been concealed from the manager, his reaction, after receiving the call, was to call immediately for his superintendent of customer relations and ask for an explanation. After this meeting the branch manager issued the following memo:

```
To:        Supt. Customer Relations    Date: 12.8.9_

From:      Branch Manager              Ref:  DE/223

Subject: The Immediate Reporting of Incidents
         Involving Customers


The branch is facing involvement in a long and
complicated enquiry by the Central Bank
investigating an incident which occurred in your
department. This has arisen as a result of the
behaviour of two tellers after a problem with a
customer had taken place.

The main reason for this situation is that neither
of the men would accept responsibility for an error,
and each tried to blame the other. A prolonged
argument ensued, in which the customer also became
involved. No agreement was reached and a full
enquiry has been set up because the customer
reported the incident to the Central Bank.

Furthermore, it was not until the following day that
```

> I was informed of the incident by which time it was
> impossible for the Branch to prevent extensive
> Central Bank involvement. This could have been
> avoided.
>
> If similar incidents should occur in future, it
> would be appreciated if I am informed immediately,
> and if personnel do not speak to customers about
> internal and personal matters.

Now assess the following statements.

		True	False
1	The writer's aim is reflected in the subject heading.	[T]	[F]
2	The writer's aim is to recommend new customers.	[T]	[F]
3	The writer's aim is reflected in the concluding paragraph of the document.	[T]	[F]
4	The writer's aim is reflected in the introductory paragraph of the document.	[T]	[F]
5	The writer's Conclusion, Aim and Subject Heading are all the same.	[T]	[F]

Answers 1T, 2F, 3T, 4F, 5T

Now express the following aims as conclusions. Note that you have already formulated the subject headings in a previous exercise (page 45).

1 To warn people who are not using their allocated parking slots.
2 To order the immediate use of ID cards.
3 To recommend the installation of the laserjet printer in all departments.
4 To suggest additional training for all new graduate employees.
5 To notify employees of the immediate introduction of the new personnel medical scheme.

Now compare your versions with those below. A verbatim effort may not be your offering but there should be a close similarity.

1 Therefore all employees should park their cars in slots allocated.
2 Therefore ID cards should be worn by all personnel as from today.

3   All departments should have a laserjet printer installed to facilitate and ensure quality printing.
4   All new graduates should therefore receive this additional training.
5   The new personnel medical scheme will come into immediate effect.

Now that you have seen the relationship between the Conclusion, Aim and Subject Heading, you may not be surprised that it is known as the CASH principle. In a report that persuades, argues, proposes, suggests, recommends, etc. the Conclusion, Aim and Subject Heading are all different expressions of the same idea.

Positioning the conclusion

At this point it is worth noting another persuasive technique that is very effective: placing the conclusion immediately after the subject heading. Since the conclusion contains the aim of the report writing task, it is not surprising that many managers prefer this vital information to be placed at the beginning of the reports they must read. This practice is usually adopted in technical reports, where the reader does not require any background information in order to appreciate the principal issue.

The conventional chronology of presenting information is in step with the chronology of production. When we write we usually introduce, develop, then conclude the topic. Since the final section includes the vital information it is not unusual for this to be placed either at the beginning or immediately after the introduction. When a reader is waiting for this information, in other words, when the document is one of many within the same departmental network, then this is not only an acceptable practice but one to be recommended.

Labelling

Besides the CASH principle, which relates to the label we have called *the subject heading*, there is also another principle which deals with labels—and an effective writer uses labels frequently to assist the reader through the document. This principle is called 'The Principle of the Flying Horse'.

If you said to a child that you were going to tell her a story of a flying horse, no matter how good your story, your voice, your intonation patterns and your own involvement may be—unless that story contained reference to a flying horse it would be judged by the child to be a very poor story indeed. Try it!

One of the principles of effective communication is not to shock and stun but to be constantly preparing your reader—or audience—to understand (not necessarily agree with) the meaning of your message. To do this requires the operation of a cognitive skill—meaningful reading or attentive listening. If your reader or audience has simultaneously to arouse another cognitive operation, that of enquiring, questioning, conjecturing or relating, this added mental burden will interfere with the reading or listening operation and therefore make the task far more difficult. Now anything that makes the reader's task more difficult must be avoided. This has already been emphasized. The reason the child did not like your story, no matter how fine and fanciful you may have thought it yourself, was because she thought she was going to hear about the horse, she was ready for it, she was waiting for it because you had used a principle of effective communication: you had prepared her for the flying horse.

Now how does this relate to report writing? First, it is far easier for your readers to assimilate the information if you limit them to one cognitive operation. Second, you must make sure that *all* your labels are direct, to the point and relevant to what follows.

Note the effectiveness/ineffectiveness of the labels—subject heading and subheading—in the following memo from an investment analyst to his manager who has required a synopsis of Gold Star technology.

```
To:      Rod Peach                Date: 29.9.9_

From:    Sid Muir                 Ref:  LBC/67

Subject: Gold Star Technology


1. Introduction

   Gold Star is a supplier of technological
   documentation. It has an impressive track record
   with 13 years of increasing profits.


2. Growth

   These results are for the year to 30.6.9_.

   Turnover:          £11.9m (£10.2m) + 17%
   Pre-tax Profits:   £1.80m (£1.63m) + 10%
   Stated Earnings:   23.3p (20.0p) + 17%
   Final Dividend:    4.4p (4.0p) + 10%
```

```
Share Price:        373p
Mkt. Cap.:          £18.9m
1989 High:          398p. Low: 248p
PE Ratio:           16. Yield: 2.4%
```

3. Computer Hardware

   This growth came from the engineering design
   field where the business is benefiting from a
   £350,000 spend on computer hardware in 19__ and
   a further £25m in 19__.

4. Explanation of Figures

   Over the last twelve months Ministry of
   Defence-related work has shrunk from over 60% to
   just under 50%. Nevertheless as the data above
   indicates there has been an overall increase of
   17%. Furthermore, this shift in market areas has
   squeezed margins. Therefore, Gold Star's goal of
   creating a European-wide technical support group
   is still feasible.

5. Future Directions

   This year the company wants to increase its
   involvement in software and expand its work in
   the automotive industry. With its present
   liquidity position it is on line to manage
   acquisitions necessary for these moves.

6. Conclusion

   The current PE ratio represents reasonable value.

Now assess the relevance of what follows in relation to the subject heading and subheadings Sid Muir has used.

	Appropriate	
	Yes	*No*
Subject heading: Gold Star Technology	[Y]	[N]
1 Introduction	[Y]	[N]
2 Growth	[Y]	[N]

		Appropriate	
		Yes	*No*
3	Computer Hardware	[Y]	[N]
4	Explanation of Figures	[Y]	[N]
5	Future Directions	[Y]	[N]
6	Conclusion	[Y]	[N]

Rewrite all the labels you think inappropriate, then compare with the following:

Subject heading: Synopsis of Gold Star Technology

1 Overview
2 Financial Results
3 Growth in 19__/__
4 Turnover Change
5 Future Directions
6 Conclusion

Summary

To project *any* image in a communicative situation you must have an *aim* that is specific, attainable and results-oriented. This applies particularly to your writing tasks if you wish them to make an indelible projection of a successful image.

This aim must become quickly apparent to your reader, especially if your document is to persuade the reader towards accepting a new idea, policy or way of thinking. There is no space for superfluous data: your argumentative discourse must begin immediately to take your reader logically and without difficulty through your text to a conclusion that cannot reasonably be resisted.

You will prepare your reader for your arguments by a delicate but forceful subject heading which will be formulated in such a way that your reader's whole analytical and diagnostic skills will be centred, not on a wasted cognitive exercise of perplexity and bewilderment, but on the inescapable inducement of your argument.

5 Making logical sections

The production process in document creation is very much determined by the initiating circumstances. Many reports are part of the work-system: monthly progress reports, marketing records and minutes of meetings fall into this category. The raw material is there waiting to be processed as a writing task. Projects which are freshly initiated either by yourself or some other authority generally rely on an initial hunt for the raw material. Take the occasion when someone says 'Look, I'd like you to look into ... and report back accordingly' or 'Do you think you could analyse and investigate, then put your observations on paper?' Or the initiative may come from yourself; you may be prompted by circumstances to say 'This is serious/interesting; I'd better investigate thoroughly and report my findings.'

Approaches to document production

As a report writer you will need to conduct an operational task. This can then be reported in the report writing tasks, e.g. a marketing trip, a meeting, monthly or daily logs. The raw material should then be processed through systematic stages. On occasions the operational task is, in fact, an integral part of the systematic stages. You may not have the raw material to process, e.g. an investigation, a comparative cost projection of two or three undecided options, an evaluation of training facilities offered by hotels in a particular city. As Figure 5.1 shows, whether the information is ready for processing or needs to be sought, both approaches require a four phase approach.

Once you realize that you must produce a report and you want to ensure it is a first-class creation, you will require a very systematic approach. Writing for success is not simply a matter of putting pen to paper. You must first do a lot of thinking and planning. In fact, if these two phases, thinking and planning, are conducted meticulously, the writing phase should be both smooth and effortless: your mind will be engaged not so much on *what* you should write but on *how* it should be

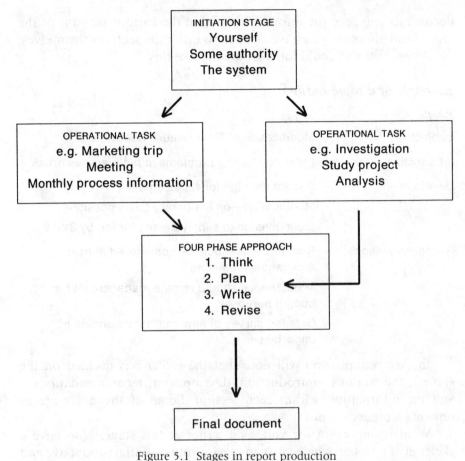

Figure 5.1 Stages in report production

written. In other words, you can devote your efforts to searching for that correct phrase, that little elusive nuance, that perfect touch for achieving excellence.

To be released to enjoy such freedom while writing is a blessing for any author. However, as a business writer, you must pay for this latitude by ensuring that all the necessary information has been gathered, selected, grouped and ordered to achieve your purpose with the reader(s) addressed.

Topic outline

We referred in Chapter 1 to the outcome of the thinking and planning stage as the **topic outline**. This is essentially a skeleton of the final document. It is a framework for the report showing how you have decided to sequence the information within the various sections of the report and also how you have decided to order the sections themselves.

A topic outline could look something like this:

Example of a topic outline

Sections	Notes
Subject:	Modification of Temperature Controllers
Introduction:	– Presently having problems in main access areas.
Development:	– Budget too high for replacement.
	– Modification—on temporary basis possible.
	– Elect division to supply details for job by 31.3.9_.
Recommendations:	– Replacement should be considered at next maintenance meeting.
	– Maintenance should remind management for budget purposes.
	– Detailed survey of new controllers should be undertaken.

In this example you will note that the writer has decided on the subject, the sections—introduction, development, recommendations—and the information within each section. Some of the notes are in sentences, others are not.

What is important for you, as a writer at this stage, is to have a skeleton of notes on which you can release your essential productive and artistic writing skills. To achieve this outcome let us examine the first two phases of the writing task: thinking and planning.

Thinking

What information will be required to make your document effective? The answer to this question is determined by your answers to the questions *why?* and *who?*

It is important to think of these three questions:

Why am I writing this paper? → AIM

Who will be my reader? → READER

What will be the information → INFORMATION
that will satisfy both?

You must ensure that the reader is exposed only to that information which is necessary and sufficient for you to achieve your aim. This first phase should, in normal circumstances, take only a matter of seconds. The point emphasized here is that no matter how routine you may find a writing task, it is always necessary to ask the *why, who* and *what.*

Consider Jim Platt, an insurance inspector for a national insurance company. Jim was given the task of reporting on a claim made by one of their clients—Scaffolding International—after an accident involving injuries to men while erecting scaffolding for a roof maintenance operation.

How long do you think it will take Jim to complete the first phase of the writing task: **thinking**?

Seconds [ ]   Minutes [ ]   Hours [ ]

Consider Hans Volker, the information technology vice-president of the consumer products division of a Danish multinational. When chairing a divisional meeting he asked one of his top managers, Ben Rogers, to assess a centralized management information system which he had lately created. This system had to satisfy the requirements of national and international units plus headquarters' requirements for immediate data for strategic planning and world forecasting.

How long do you think it will take Ben to complete the first phase of the writing task: **thinking**?

Seconds [ ]   Minutes [ ]   Hours [ ]

Consider: You have just been on a three-day professional training course. On completion of the programme your immediate boss asks for a course report.

How long do you think it will take you to complete the first phase of the writing task: **thinking**?

Seconds [ ]   Minutes [ ]   Hours [ ]

Yes, for all three scenarios the writer will take only *seconds* to realize the aim, reader and information.

Planning

In the scenarios above, the three writers, once they have identified the information required to satisfy their readers and aims, will start to *gather* and *select* the necessary factual information. This must then be *grouped* and *sequenced*, together with the non-factual information, i.e. the interpretations, opinions, recommendations, conclusions, etc.

This is the most difficult phase of the writing process. A case study will verify this and will also help you to appreciate the exertion required.

Case study

Eddie Bolang is senior investment manager (Agriculture) for a European investment group. For several months he has been studying the possibility of capital investment in the (fictitious) state of Zahrain. Eddie had to travel to the Arabian Gulf and interview many people at government level in order to produce a report to provide sufficient information for his general manager to form a policy for investment in the Zahraini Agricultural Development Scheme (ZADS).

Eddie has gathered the following 32 pieces of information. Study each carefully then assess the statements that follow.

1   The 1000-strong herd of Friesian heifers is the only indigenous bulk supplier of fresh milk: 4000 to 6000 litres a day.
2   Government policy is to achieve self-sufficiency in agriculture and further expand the agricultural section.
3   Annual production capacity should be increased to 3.2 million broilers and 36 million table eggs by the end of the year because of the new extension.
4   Many flocks are quite small and Zahrain remains dependent on the importation of live animals.
5   Zahrain is due to develop as a tourist attraction during the 1990s.
6   Summer temperatures rise to 50°C with a winter low of 7°C. Humidity can be as high as 100 per cent.
7   Most milk bought in Zahrain is reconstituted from imported milk powder.
8   Investment in new technology has government backing and last year's figures for domestic production are encouraging.
9   Current demand is for 11 million broilers and 70 million table eggs.
10   There is a definite need for investment in all areas of agriculture studied.
11   Notwithstanding a steady increase in sport, Zahrain does not have a national cricket team.
12   The population is centred mainly in Zahrain capital city.
13   A report had to be submitted six months later: 23 December 1990.
14   Tomatoes, aubergines, onions, cucumbers, dates and melons are the principal crops.
15   There is a 600-hectare government farm to the north of the island with 6000 adult breeding ewes and over 10 000 other animals.

16 More than 300 000 head of sheep from Australia were imported in the first half of 1990.
17 The general position is likely to change when the government dairy farm begins production in 1991.
18 The government poultry farm is located 36 kilometres north of Zahrain capital city.
19 The objectives are to supply farmers with good quality animals and experiment with new forage crops capable of withstanding the Zahraini climate.
20 The 3.2-hectare Wafrah Greenhouse Project produces 1000 tonnes of different vegetables a year.
21 The average rainfall is 70–90 mm a year (winter season).
22 At the annual review meeting on 23 June 1990, it was decided to investigate the opportunities for investment in agriculture in Zahrain.
23 In total there are 50 000 sheep in the country.
24 Only one dairy farm—the Zahrain Dairy Company—operates on anything approaching a commercial basis.
25 The farm has an annual production capacity of 1 million broilers and 10 million table eggs.
26 Production is now continuous throughout the year due to climate-controlled greenhouses.
27 Production of fruit and vegetables accounts for 34 per cent of Zahrain's agricultural income.
28 The farm produces a small quantity of mutton for the local market.
29 Despite a steady rise in local production Zahrain's imports of fruit and vegetables in 1989 were 28 per cent up on 1988.
30 Zahrain occupies an arid island of 10 600 square kilometres.
31 Of the total population of 250 000 only 60 000 are Zahrainis.
32 The principal areas for investigation were:
   a. fruit and vegetables
   b. sheep
   c. milk and dairy products
   d. poultry and eggs

Now assess these statements.

		True	False
1	The information is in logical order.	[T]	[F]
2	Some pieces of information seem to share a similar theme or idea.	[T]	[F]

		True	False
3	All 32 pieces of information are necessary for Eddie to achieve his aim.	[T]	[F]
4	Several pieces could be grouped under the heading Conclusions.	[T]	[F]
5	It would be easier for the reader to assimilate this information if it were grouped and labelled.	[T]	[F]

Answers 1F, 2T, 3F, 4T, 5T

Eddie decides to use the following headings for the different sections of his report.

```
1.0  Introduction

2.0  Geographical Considerations

3.0  Population

4.0  Agricultural Production

     4.1  Fruit and Vegetables

     4.2  Sheep

     4.3  Milk and Dairy Products

     4.4  Poultry and Eggs

5.0 Conclusions
```

Which points in Eddie's notes should be included under which heading in his report? (*Note*: Do not include any points under the general heading 4.0 Agricultural Production, only under its subheadings.) Once you have completed the exercise, compare your views with those presented below.

1.0	Introduction	2, 8, 13, 22, 32
2.0	Geographical Considerations	6, 21, 30
3.0	Population	12, 31
4.0	Agricultural Production	
	4.1 Fruit and Vegetables	14, 20, 26, 27, 29

4.2	Sheep	4, 15, 16, 19, 23, 28
4.3	Milk and Dairy Products	1, 7, 17, 24
4.4	Poultry and Eggs	3, 9, 18, 25
5.0	Conclusions	10

How does your attempt compare with the model presented? If it is not exactly the same, then you as a writer would need to be able to justify adequately your reasons for including each piece of information under the headings given.

Grouping

In practice, you would probably start the grouping activity during the gathering exercise. Whatever process you use, you will group according to the information you have selected. And then you will order, as we have noted, according to reader expectancies, maximizing your potential for the reader to accept your purpose.

The grouping stage in the planning phase is determined essentially by the information you have decided is necessary and sufficient for achieving your aim with the identified readership.

Writers who do not plan properly tend to confuse their readers by putting recommendations in the middle of discussions or giving reasons for purchasing a machine in the middle of the description. This practice can be very annoying. It is like having a grocery list with shampoo in the middle of the carrots, onions, celery, tomatoes and cucumber!

If Eddie Bolang had not given himself the groupings he did, his report would have been very difficult to assimilate. The groupings that he used:

Introduction
Geographical Considerations
Population
Agricultural Production
    Fruit and Vegetables
    Sheep
    Milk and Dairy Products
    Poultry and Eggs
Conclusions

were based on the **information** he had gathered which, in turn, as we have seen, is determined by the aim and reader.

Ordering

The criteria for ordering the pockets of information in a report will depend ultimately on the type of document you have to produce, given these three variables: reader, aim, information.

Here are some examples.

Order of importance

e.g. Leaving the strongest argument until the last to support your conclusions.

e.g. Placing the strongest argument at the beginning to arouse a sense of urgency in your reader.

These examples have the reader variable exerting the most influence.

Order depending on location

e.g.   A marketing report or a report on various locations in a plant.

Both reports could have groupings based on chronology of locations visited e.g. 1st France, 2nd Belgium, 3rd The Netherlands and finally Germany.

Order relating cause and effect

e.g.   An accident report where the effects of the incident may rely on an appreciation of the causes (or vice versa).

Here the ordering criterion is logic.

Order depending on urgency of information

e.g.   A professional opinion is required immediately by the reader and any supportive information becomes secondary.

Here the ordering decision is a matter of common sense and expediency.

Order determined by the logical sequence of the groupings

e.g. A report arguing that a policy should not be introduced in its present form would require:
- 1st—the argument in favour of the policy
- 2nd—the argument against the policy, leading to
- 3rd—the conclusion *not* to introduce.

Let us review a few scenarios to see how these ordering principles apply to different situations.

Scenario one

Tom Gower works in the sales department of a UK organization that produces car accessories for export to mainland Europe.

Departmental meetings are held on the first Friday of each month to review the previous month's activities. Tom feels that this is far too early. He writes to his boss: his aim is to propose that monthly meetings are held on the third Friday of each month. He marshalls his information into the following groups. What sequence should be used to maximize his chances of successfully achieving his aim?

A All arguments in favour of meetings held on the third Friday of each month.
B Explanation of the present schedule for monthly meetings.
C Conclusion that all monthly meetings should be held on the third Friday of each month.
D All arguments against meetings being held on the first Friday of each month.

The most logical sequence would be **B, D, A, C.**

B is a form of introduction.
D dismisses the negative arguments against the proposal.
A highlights the positive arguments to lead to ...
C a positive conclusion.

The sequence is determined in this case by the writer's *aim* which is expressed in the conclusion.

Scenario two

The aims of the two texts which follow are the same. The conclusions are therefore the same and the information is the same. The only difference is that one of the writers did not let the aim determine the sequence: he therefore produces an ineffective document. Can you identify which is which?

Text A

> ADMINISTRATION OF DRUG XZEPHERITE
>
> The drug Xzepherite has lately proved very successful in prolonging the life of several sufferers of Xzepheritis. This is mainly due to modifications made by Dr Xzepher and his research assistant Xzepheras. The case in Tokyo of Mr Yoshiki Takahashi in 1984 was reported at the International Medical Annual Review Conference of 1985. The following year three cases from the United States and four from Europe were all reported as successful. In fact, for the last five years there have been no negative reports on this drug. Despite experiments failing when several patients died from its initial administration, it is concluded that the Xzepherite drug can go into general circulation.

Text B

> ADMINISTRATION OF THE DRUG XZEPHERITE
>
> Despite experiments failing when several patients died from its initial administration, the drug Xzepherite has lately proved very successful in prolonging the life of several sufferers of Xzepheritis. This is mainly due to modifications made by Dr Xzepher and his research assistant Xzepheras. The case in Tokyo of Mr Yoshiki Takahashi in 1984 was reported at the International Medical Annual Review Conference of 1985. The following year three cases from the United States and four from Europe were all reported as successful. In fact, for the last five years there have been no negative reports on this drug. It is concluded that the Xzepherite drug can go into general circulation.

The writer of document A would hardly achieve his aim by placing the strong argument *against* his proposal immediately before the conclusion!

Scenario three

The following is a letter from the Central Bank of Medland to the general manager of one of the commercial banks. What ordering criterion did the writer employ in this case?

Dear Sir,

EXAMINATION OF BANK XYZ

We appreciate the courtesy extended to our examiners. A study of their report has been undertaken.

Since the last inspection no progress has been noted regarding:

— the accounting system
— internal control
— housekeeping

You are urged to take appropriate action on these matters immediately.

Please keep us advised.

Yours faithfully

Here the ordering criterion of cause and effect has been followed.

Scenario four

To: Bill Binders   Date: 12.8.19__
         Chief Executive and
         General Manager

From: Art Bowman   Ref: MPD/GML/9/AR
         Manager, Data Processing

Subject: Purchase of Software Modules (Personal Computers)

Reference is made to our discussion in your office yesterday, 11 August 19__.

In order to allow the personal computers to be

linked together in a multi-user environment we need
to purchase the following software modules:

Multiple Office Activities   – US$ 3250/–
4 G/L Application Generator   – US$ 3250/–

I shall be grateful if you could kindly authorize
this purchase.

Art Bowman
Manager, Data Processing

Here the ordering principle is logic.

Review exercise

Jim Bellamy is the officer in charge (OIC) of an inspection team of the
auditing department at the headquarters of a banking group. After a
spot check with his team of inspectors, he has decided that the
operations in the Mainland branch are not ideal. He writes down all the
items he must report: these include not only the facts he has *gathered*
and *selected* but also his interpretations and opinions. He randomly
notes down these 20 points.

1   In the interest of service to customers the Cash Receipts counter
    should be extended by making one of the paying cashiers assist
    Teller No. 1.
2   This report will be addressed to the manager of operations.
3   This inspection was limited to the Cash Department.
4   At close of business on 12.4.91 cash on hand was physically
    checked and compared with the general ledger balance of the day.
    No discrepancy was identified for any of the tellers:
    No. 1   US$ 458,243.020
    No. 2   US$ 245,329.000
    No. 3   US$ 614,761.290
    No. 4   On leave
5   The Cash Department was inspected on 12.4.91.
6   Tellers should behave more courteously to all customers.
7   Generally the department is well managed. Principal procedures
    are followed according to bank policy. However, unnecessary and
    obsolete forms, papers, etc. were stacked on the floor and on
    shelves in the strong room. This is both dangerous and untidy.

8   All unwanted and unnecessary documents should be destroyed.

9   All tellers seem to work well together. However, an abruptness with minor customers was observed.

10   The petty cash register should be completed daily and the balance agreed to and signed by the OIC.

11   All items were checked. There was a complete agreement with the respective registers maintained by the OIC.

12   It was observed that a long queue of depositors was always present at the counter of Teller No. 1. Each customer was subjected to at least a 15-minute delay.

13   It was observed that payments effective from 4.4.91 had not been recorded in the petty cash register. Payments were therefore identified and vouchers written out. The cash on hand subsequently balanced.

14   Except during month-beginning/month-end the paying cashiers (Tellers 2 and 3) were not fully engaged during banking hours. On average they dealt with about 60 payments during the four hours.

15   Teller No. 1 is responsible for cash receipts for:
     - Current Accounts
     - Savings Bank
     - Fixed Deposits
     - General Ledger

16   The petty cash at close of business on 12.4.91, held by Teller No. 2, was physically counted and agreed with the general ledger.

17   Gold Bullion   )
     Travellers Cheques   ) These items were
     Safe Custody Documents: Customers   ) in safe custody.
     Safe Custody Documents: Bank   )

18   It was observed that the manager of the main branch did not carry out any 'surprise checks' during January and March, 1991 (refer Cash Department Procedure, page 4, paragraph 2(b)).

19   The inspection covered the following staff:
     1 officer-in-charge
     4 tellers
     1 clerk
     2 cleaners

20   Books, records, cash, safe, including custody items, were all inspected.

   Arrange these 20 points into groups that share a similar theme or idea and label each group. You can then compare your effort with the report presented below.

To: Manager, Operations   Date: 19 May 19__

From: Officer-in-Charge,   Ref: MO/INSP/GENL/5/91
       Inspection Team

AUDIT INSPECTION: CASH DEPARTMENT

1.0 INTRODUCTION

The Cash Department was inspected on 12.4.91.
The inspection covered:

1.1 Staff: Officer-in-Charge (1)
    Tellers   (4)
    Clerk   (1)
    Cleaners   (2)
1.2 Books
1.3 Records
1.4 Cash
1.5 Safe, including custody items.

2.0 CASH ON HAND

At close of business on 12.4.91 this was
physically checked and compared with the general
ledger balance of the day. No discrepancy was
identified for any of the tellers:

No. 1 US $ 458,243.020
No. 2 US $ 245,329.000
No. 3 US $ 614,761.290
No. 4 On leave

Total US $ 1,318,333.310

3.0 PETTY CASH

The balance at close of business on 12.4.91,
held by Teller No. 2, was physically counted and
agreed with the general ledger.

It was observed that payments effective from
4.4.91 had not been recorded in the petty cash

register. Payments were therefore identified and
vouchers written out. The cash on hand
subsequently balanced.

4.0 CASH TRANSACTIONS

4.1 Teller No. 1

Teller No. 1 is responsible for cash
receipts for:

— Current Accounts
— Savings Bank
— Fixed Deposits
— General Ledger

It was observed that a long queue of
depositors was always present in front of
his counter. Each customer was subjected to
at least a 15-minute delay.

4.2 Tellers No. 2 and No. 3

Except during month-beginning/month-end the
paying cashiers were not fully engaged
during banking hours. On average they were
dealing with about 60 payments during the
four hours.

5.0 CUSTOMER RELATIONS

All tellers seem to work well together. However,
an abruptness with some minor customers was
observed.

6.0 ITEMS IN SAFE CUSTODY

These can be divided into four:

— Gold Bullion
— Travellers Cheques
— Safe Custody Documents: Customers
— Safe Custody Documents: Bank

All items were checked. There was a complete
agreement with the respective registers
maintained by the OIC.

7.0 SPOT CHECKS

It was observed that the Manager of the main
branch did not carry out any 'surprise checks'
during January and March, 1991 (refer Cash
Department Procedure, page 4, paragraph 2(b)).

8.0 CONCLUSIONS

Generally the department is well managed.
Principal procedures are followed according to
Bank policy. However, unnecessary and obsolete
forms, papers, etc. were stacked on the floor
and on shelves in the strong room. This is both
dangerous and untidy.

9.0 RECOMMENDATIONS

9.1 The petty cash register should be completed
daily and the balance agreed to and signed
by the OIC.

9.2 In the interest of service to customers the
Cash Receipts counter should be extended by
making one of the paying cashiers assist
Teller No. 1.

9.3 Tellers should behave more courteously to
all customers.

9.4 All unwanted and unnecessary documents
should be destroyed.

Summary

In this chapter you have examined the main determining factors for
gathering, selecting, grouping and ordering information. The two most
important factors remain your purpose and the reader, but when it
comes to ordering the groups of information one must be practical—the

information itself may be a crucial factor. Depending on the type of report and other pragmatic issues, a sequence for the material could be determined by:

- importance to reader/aim
- cause and effect relationship
- expediency/urgency
- location
- time
- logic

Once you have ordered your groupings under appropriate headings, you should feel free to concentrate on the language aspects of your report, especially tone and style.

6 Using an appropriate tone

There are times in our commercial documents when we make pre-
dictions yet cannot be categorically certain of our facts; for
example, when we are making plans or forecasts. Geologists,
medical doctors and even politicians cannot always write with certainty. On other occasions, when reporting past events or current
situations, we ought to be explicit, clear and frank. We can call the
former scenarios tentative, the latter, direct. Now the language
phenomena in this distinction are respectively the same as those for
when we are addressing an authority (tentative) and when we are
addressing a subordinate (direct). Obviously, we need to acquaint
and equip ourselves with the language techniques applicable for all
possible scenarios. In other words, we require the linguistic proficiency to create the tone to match the occasion.

Tone: the human factor

Business documents are usually formal and exact in terms of relaying
information about facts, figures and findings. There can be something
very scientific and distant in the impact they radiate; indeed, with the
modern emphasis on speed and electrification, the human element is fast
becoming inconsequential. Nevertheless, no matter how distant we mere
humans may become from the internal cogs of the international communication machine, our assessments and evaluations are still weighty and
powerful in the last resort. The effects and the causes are still human in
nature; witness the stock market calamity of 1987: computers were
blamed but we felt the effects.

So it is with your business exchanges. The corporate client in Japan
and/or the customer account in Venezuela are both represented by
people, with feelings and aches, with problems and setbacks, with
families and homes. In other words, the business entity is represented by
a person who has a personal and private emotive element. It is sup-
pressed through training because of corporate objectives but is nevertheless poised like a quivering arrow on a fully stretched bow. Make

certain that your document does not occasion any resoundingly negative response. The consequences of that inept choice of phrase or silly innuendo, that tactless mistake, could be insurmountable for you and, in some cases, your organization.

The point here is that in the final analysis you are communicating, even in business, with other *people*. If you want their reaction to be positive and in line with your desires you must diplomatically select the words which will effect this response.

Case study one

Let us presume that you work in the research and development division of Europa Chemicals. As manager of food and beverages you delegate much of your work to your section heads. One of your section leaders is Anne Sherwood, who has only lately joined your division. She is technically an asset to the department but she does tend to be a little over-zealous and bossy. Indeed, her ambitious behaviour could oust you from your managerial position!

One day she sends you the following memo.

To: Manager, Food and Beverages

From: Section Leader: Electro Analysis

Date: 23.8.9_

Subject: RK6 Food Additive

Despite my recommendation to dispense with the RK6 and work on the new SQ3 you still insist on the former. This is definitely a wrong decision.

Unless you can supply any technical reasons to support the RK6 I must insist that the SQ3 forms the basis of my future work in this area.

I will be at the Electro Analysis Conference on Monday. However, if you have any further comments to make on this issue I shall be in my office on Tuesday morning.

Anne Sherwood.

Indicate your reaction to this memo.

		Yes	No
1	This memo has made me feel annoyed.	[Y]	[N]
2	Anne should show more respect in her memo—especially to me, her boss.	[Y]	[N]
3	This is a technical matter so emotions are of little importance: Anne has used the correct tone.	[Y]	[N]
4	Anne certainly knows how to cajole me into changing my mind.	[Y]	[N]
5	Anne can use an authoritative tone because she is technically correct.	[Y]	[N[
6	Even if Anne is technically correct the tone of this memo is not correct.	[Y]	[N]

Answers 1Y, 2Y, 3N, 4N, 5N, 6Y

Any communication—oral or written—can be analysed on two aspects: the factual information and the affective information content of the message.

The following sentence pairs have the same factual content.

a. Would it be possible for you to send me the report as early as possible?
b. Get that report to me immediately.

a. Payroll and time accounting changes will come into effect as from 3 August 1992.
b. Payroll and time accounting changes should come into effect as from 3 August 1992.

a. It is possible that the software might not suit our requirements.
b. The software will not suit our requirements.

Each sentence pair expresses the same concept. *What* is expressed is labelled the *factual content*.

However, the concept in the first sentence of each pair is expressed in a completely different way from the second sentence. *How* it is expressed is called the *affective content*.

In a commercial setting you write to get things done (or not done in some cases). You want the aim of your document to be realized, to be achieved, to be acted upon. If this is the case, the affective content of your texts will need to be carefully and diplomatically worded, for this stimulates the nature of the responsive force.

Would you have reacted in a different way if Anne Sherwood had produced the following:

```
To:       Manager, Food and Beverages

From:     Section Leader: Electro Analysis

Date:     23.8.9_

Subject: RK6 Food Additive

It is generally acknowledged by most electro
analysts that the new S 3 additive will replace the
RK6. Although I do respect your ideas about the RK6
I would like to discuss this topic more fully next
week. Perhaps I could then present my ideas about
the S 3.

I shall be at the Electro Analysis Conference in
Brussels on Monday so would it be possible for me to
see you on Tuesday morning?
```

What Anne Sherwood expressed here is exactly the same as the first document: the *factual content* is the same. However, how this is expressed is completely different: i.e. it has a different *affective content*.

If your reaction to the latter document was different from your reaction to Anne's earlier effort, then your change in attitude must be a result of the affective content. The affective content is therefore very important for it changes what we can refer to as the **tone** of the document. You will sometimes need to use one tone, sometimes another. What is important for you now is to know that there are language devices available to enable you to achieve whatever tone you require.

Tone: the language factor

The three principal language devices are:
- the use of a particular type of verb referred to as a modal. Note the change in tone through the modal verb in the following sentences:
  - You *are* to stop smoking.
  - You *must* stop smoking.
  - You *should* stop smoking.
  - You *could* stop smoking.

- the use of certain introductory phrases for effect. Note the change in tone through the use of the introductory phrase, e.g.:
  - Get me a cup of tea.
  - *Would it be possible for you* to get me a cup of tea?
  - This is not correct.
  - *It is possible that* this is not correct.
  - The currency values will change.
  - *It is likely that* the currency values will change.
- the difference in choice of vocabulary.

To demonstrate the change in tone, and assess your appreciation of these changes, you should now carefully read the following two texts and assess the evaluation statements which follow each.

The following memo is from the Inspection Division of a retail business.

Subject: <u>Proposed Rescheduling of Auditing</u>
         <u>Procedures</u>

The effectiveness and frequency at which auditing procedures are carried out are being reviewed.

With present policy, all branches are examined every three months. We are requested to produce a full detailed report before and after all examinations.

With the degree of permanently installed, sophisticated monitoring equipment, combined in many cases with proven long-running periods without problems, these examinations are superfluous. We will lengthen such auditing intervals in most cases to six months.

The timetable for the less reliable or manual operations will not be changed but the intervals for computerized operations will be lengthened.

Thank you for your cooperation.

	True	*False*
The writer is making a recommendation.	[T]	[F]
The writer is requesting a change of policy.	[T]	[F]
The auditing procedures will certainly change.	[T]	[F]

	True	*False*
The writer has authority to change the auditing procedures.	[T]	[F]
The reader's opinion is of no concern to the writer.	[T]	[F]

Now read this memo, which has the same factual information as the first:

Subject: <u>Proposed Rescheduling of Auditing Procedures</u>

We would like to review the effectiveness and frequency at which auditing procedures are currently carried out.

It is presently the policy to examine all branches every three months. In addition, we are normally requested to produce a full detailed report before and after all examinations.

It is possible that, with the degree of permanently installed, sophisticated monitoring equipment, combined in many cases with proven long-running periods without problems, that such frequent examinations could be considered to be superfluous. It is suggested that it would appear appropriate to lengthen the auditing intervals in most cases to six months.

It is not proposed that the timetable for the less reliable or manual operations be changed. However, would it be possible to consider lengthening the intervals for computerized operations?

Your comments on these proposals would be appreciated.

	True	*False*
The writer is making a recommendation.	[T]	[F]
The writer is requesting a change of policy.	[T]	[F]
The auditing procedures will certainly change.	[T]	[F]

	True	*False*
The writer has authority to change the auditing procedures.	[T]	[F]
The reader's opinion is of no concern to the writer.	[T]	[F]

Your answers to the first exercise should read F, F, T, T, T and the opposite T, T, F, F, F for the second. Why should this be so?

In industry and commerce, your writing must achieve a particular aim, which is generally to:

- get people to change their minds to your way of thinking;
- accept your recommendation, proposal, suggestion;
- act on your order;
- provide the information requested.

It is essential, therefore, that the reader's reaction is exactly as you anticipate. Every message conveys two types of information content—factual and affective—and one's reaction as a reader will invariably be to the affective information content, as in the case of the earlier Anne Sherwood scenario.

The affective content of a message can complement either the relationship of you as the writer to the reader in terms of authority, or the degree of certainty/doubt you have about your topic. In other words, the affective information content carries the tone in terms of either authority or certainty.

If you have authority, or if you are writing with a degree of certainty regarding your topic, then your *tone* can be downward, direct and hard.

Consider the affective content of the following sentences:

1   Answer the attached letter.
2   Be in my office at 9 o'clock in the morning.
3   Valves AB and AC are closed.
4   There will be a new exchange rate.
5   Visas are not required for UK citizens.

If you do not have authority, or if you are writing with a degree of uncertainty regarding your topic, then your tone will be upward, tentative and soft.

Consider the change in the affective content of these sentences expressing the same factual information as those just reviewed.

1   Would you please answer the attached letter?
2   Would it be possible for you to be in my office at 9 o'clock tomorrow morning?
3   Valves AB and AC may be closed.

4   There could be a new exchange rate.
5   Visas could be required for UK citizens.

To appreciate the downward and direct tone, identify those sentences below where the writer has authority and therefore uses a direct tone, and/or where the writer is expressing facts and therefore also uses a direct tone.

1   All high speed survey intervals will be lengthened.
2   Visas are required to enter the country.
3   Meetings are held in the conference room on the first Friday of every month.
4   A careful selection of chemicals will ensure no damage to the formation.
5   Coffee break is at 11 o'clock.
6   Send the report tomorrow.
7   The contractor shall ensure that all workers are qualified.
8   Only authorized personnel are permitted beyond this point.
9   All employees must carry their ID card at all times.
10   The letters are ready for the manager's signature.

The *tone* or impact of the message for each of these sentences is strong, hard and direct. This tone can be used when the writer:
●   has authority as in sentences 1, 2, 6, 7, 8, 9, or
●   is expressing certainty as in sentences 3, 4, 5 and 10.

Now identify those sentences below where the writer does not have authority and therefore uses a tentative tone, and/or where the writer is uncertain of the facts and therefore also uses a tentative tone.

1   Would it be possible to survey the area tomorrow?
2   It is likely that working in a high-noise environment without ear defenders for any length of time may lead to permanent hearing disability.
3   Disciplinary measures might then be taken against those who fail to comply.
4   It is possible that a training programme could be developed to company specifications.
5   An alarm system might be the answer to our problems.
6   It is therefore suggested that all personnel should be made aware of the situation.
7   Samples would probably require examination before a commitment could be made to purchase.
8   Generally, these structures tend to exhibit an elongated NE/SW anticlinal trend.

9   The suspected anomaly to the southern extension could be of merit for future exploration.

10   It is apparent that reprocessing could enhance reflection components.

The tone or impact of the message for each of these sentences is weak, tentative and soft. This tone may be used when the writer does not have authority as in 1, 3, 4, 6, 7 or is expressing an idea about which he cannot be 100 per cent certain as in 2, 5, 8, 9, 10. The last three sentences are taken from a seismic survey report where the writer can never be fully certain of the facts.

You should now appreciate how the tone aspect of business writing is so important to the successful impact we wish to project. Let us now put your ideas to the test by considering the following case.

Case study two

Fernandes Toro is the manager of the foreign exchange division of the busy Ruwais branch of the Commercial Bank of Mainland. Fernandes has been in this position for three years and is expecting promotion in the not too distant future.

However, his colleagues in the other branches—Corniche, Crescent and Main Street—are not as strict and careful as he is about their trainee dealers. Many errors have been reported to the head office and Fernandes knows that, as last year, he will be collectively grouped with his colleagues when the issue of trainee errors is discussed at the forthcoming annual meeting. Fernandes writes to the general manager.

Which document do you think he should send to his boss—A or B?

Memorandum A

Subject: Errors by Trainee Dealers

An alarming increase in the number of errors by trainee dealers has recently been noted. On each occasion, the error occurred when the dealer was working without supervision.

Such errors will be avoided if strict levels of supervision are maintained. In future, an experienced dealer must be present at all times when a trainee is carrying out operational duties. If further errors occur, responsibility will rest with the Branch Manager in charge of the trainee.

Memorandum B

```
Subject: Errors by Trainee Dealers

Many trainee dealers have made errors at work in
recent weeks, and it seems that, on each occasion,
the error occurred when the dealer was working
without supervision.

It is possible that such errors could be avoided if
stricter levels of supervision were maintained. It
is therefore felt that, in future, an experienced
dealer should be present at all times when a trainee
is carrying out operational duties. If further such
errors should occur, responsibility would rest with
the Branch Manager in charge of the trainee.
```

Would you agree that the first memo would not get the required reaction? It is too hard, direct and authoritative to send to the boss! The second memo is far more accommodating.

Now the factual content is the same in both documents. The affective content is different on the three language points: modal verbs, vocabulary and use of an introductory phrase.

Memorandum A	*Memorandum B*
Here, tone is expressed by strong *modal verbs*:	Here, tone is expressed by soft *modal verbs*:
is/are	can
must	should
will	may
shall	might
and the imperative 'must'	would
	could
Here, tone is expressed using *precise vocabulary*:	Here, tone is expressed using a more *decisive vocabulary*:
order	request
command	proposal
decision	proposition
now	as soon as possible

Memorandum A	*Memorandum B*
Here, the writer does not use *introductory phrases*.	Here, the message is frequently introduced by *introductory phrases*:

It is possible that ...
It is therefore felt that ...
It seems that ...

Can you differentiate between the two tones tentative and direct in these sentences?

1   Would it be possible for you to send me the figures as early as possible?   [T]   [D]

2   A recent survey shows that inflation is under control.   [T]   [D]

3   It seems that the pound might continue on this upward trend.   [T]   [D]

4   It is possible that a new emphasis on green issues may affect company policy in this regard.   [T]   [D]

5   An agreement on corporate objectives must be reached.   [T]   [D]

6   Confirmation requires additional seismic surveys.   [T]   [D]

7   Replace this software with another word processing package.   [T]   [D]

8   If the company confirms their decision to discontinue the present electronic mail system, then we should consider upgrading all terminals to complement the enhanced program.   [T]   [D]

9   This option may not be available next month.   [T]   [D]

10   Another point of convergence is in tax and benefits.   [T]   [D]

Answers 1T, 2D, 3T, 4T, 5D, 6D, 7D, 8T, 9T, 10D.

Remember the memo below, which was used in Chapter 5? It was written to Bill Binders. Art Bowman has obviously used some diplomatic skills to achieve a sense of assertion, even though he is writing to his boss. Initially we examined the memo for its ordering principle. Now let us appreciate the tone.

```
To:      Bill Binders            Date: 12.8.19__
         Chief Executive and
         General Manager

From:    Art Bowman              Ref:  MPD/GML/9/AR
         Manager, Data Processing

Subject: Purchase of Software Modules
         (Personal Computers)

Reference is made to our discussion in your office
yesterday, 11 August 19__.

In order to allow the personal computers to be
linked together in a multi-user environment we need
to purchase the following software modules:

Multiple Office Activities    - US$ 3250/-
4 G/L Application Generator    - US$ 3250/-

I shall be grateful if you could kindly authorize
this purchase.


Art Bowman
Manager, Data Processing
```

Give five language markers to indicate that *both* direct and tentative aspects have been applied.

1. _____

2. _____

3. _____

4. _____

5. _____

Here are some of the markers you could have listed.

1. Art Bowman gives a reminder of the reason for the purchase—*In order to* ... = tentative
2. *We need to purchase* = direct

3. *I shall be grateful* = direct and at the same time tentative
   Modal verb *shall* is direct; as an introductory phrase, it is also
   tentative, plus vocabulary use, i.e. *grateful*
4. *kindly* = tentative
5. *authorize* = direct.

Review exercises

Exercise one

Saleem Bakir is a senior supplier working for a major oil company
which has offshore platforms in the Arabian Gulf. It is essential that
potable water is always 'on tap'. Lately he has noticed a sudden decrease
in the stock of liquid chlorine, an essential factor in the process of
making desalinated water potable. He writes the following memo to his
section head who, like most buyers under pressure to keep costs to a
minimum, will question the validity of Saleem's request.

    Here is the memo. First study the text, then underline any modal
verb, introductory phrase or vocabulary entry which has helped Saleem
to be direct, yet respectful to authority. Compare your ideas with the
underscored version which follows.

```
To:       Purchasing Section Head

From:     Senior Buyer, Al Wasl Complex

Date:     30 September 19__

Subject:  Recommended Increase in Liquid Chlorine
          Stock
```

Since the chemical, liquid chlorine, is a very
important factor for processing drinking water there
should always be enough stock to cope with both
daily demand and emergency situations. The current
stock will only be sufficient for one month, i.e.
until the end of October.

It was noticed that consumption increased
significantly during this month which has
contributed to this urgent need to replenish stocks
as soon as possible.

Therefore in order to avoid possible problems during October it is suggested to:

- increase levels to cope with the next quarter
- identify the causes of the sudden increase in demand.

Accordingly, it is recommended:

a. that a quantity of liquid chlorine is purchased immediately to cover the rest of 19__;
b. that stock levels should be replenished on a monthly basis.

Your immediate approval would be gratefully appreciated.

To: Purchasing Section Head

From: Senior Buyer, Al Wasl Complex

Date: 30 September 19__

Subject: Recommended Increase in Liquid Chlorine Stock

Since the chemical, liquid chlorine, is a very important factor for processing drinking water there should always be enough stock to cope with both daily demand and emergency situations. The current stock will only be sufficient for one month, i.e. until the end of October.

It was noticed that consumption increased significantly during this month which has contributed to this urgent need to replenish stocks as soon as possible.

Therefore in order to avoid possible problems during October it is suggested to:

- increase levels to cope with the next quarter
- identify the causes of the sudden increase in demand.

Accordingly, it is recommended:

a. that a quantity of liquid chlorine is purchased
   immediately to cover the rest of 19__;
b. that stock levels should be replenished on a
   monthly basis.

Your immediate approval would be gratefully
appreciated.

Exercise two

Tick the appropriate box.

		Agree	*Disagree*
1	The affective content of a message can give a direct, strong and hard tone to the factual content.	[ ]	[ ]
2	The modals are verbs which express the tone of a message.	[ ]	[ ]
3	The following sentence makes a good advert for a new washing powder: 'Spinwash is a new powder which may clean all your laundry.'	[ ]	[ ]
4	Introductory phrases weaken the impact of a message.	[ ]	[ ]
5	When writing about the future financial situation, a writer ought to use a direct tone.	[ ]	[ ]
6	The affective content when issuing an order is similar to that relating to facts.	[ ]	[ ]
7	The impact of factual information can be changed by the use of: • modals • introductory phrases, and • vocabulary.	[ ]	[ ]
8	The following phrases are probably taken from a downward communication: • as soon as possible • please try to comply with these new regulations • whenever it is convenient • I would be extremely grateful.	[ ]	[ ]

Agree   Disagree

9   The following sentences become weaker by the
change of modal: [ ]   [ ]
   ● You *must* stop smoking.
   ● You *will* stop smoking.
   ● You *should* stop smoking.
   ● You *could* stop smoking.

10   The following extract is taken from a passage
that expresses a tone of uncertainty: [ ]   [ ]
There seems to be little hope of a return to
profitable activity for Phoenix, and in fact the
strategy now appears to be the gradual reduction
of the workforce. This could indicate a winding
down of this arm of the company in favour of
investment elsewhere.
Therefore, it is possible that losses could
continue for the rest of this year.

Answers 1A, 2A, 3D, 4A, 5D, 6A, 7A, 8D, 9A, 10A.

Exercise three

Now that you appreciate the three significant language techniques for
creating an appropriate tone, underline the modals, introductory
phrases and vocabulary entries in the document below that help the
writer generate the inflection required in the document. Compare with
those indicated in the key which follows.

For the interim, the positive trade news may help to
lengthen the horizon for dollar stability. Longer term,
however, the markets could remain extremely wary of the
dollar's vulnerability with the realized correction to
the trade deficit falling far short of present
expectations.

It is possible that with data releases not providing a
clear direction of economic activity, monetary policy
could remain broadly unchanged. Short-term, dollar
stability may provide a shift in policy emphasis to
maintain sufficient growth momentum for the election
year ahead, which could allow a slight softening in
rates. However, the huge funding requirement and need to

retain interest in dollar denominated assets should preclude any significant downward adjustment. Longer term, with further dollar weakness anticipated, upward pressure on rates might resume.

Despite Bank of England calls for a prudent UK budget, the Chancellor's commitment to tax cuts suggests that interest rates could remain the dominant vehicle to implement restraint. In the run-up to the budget an imminent increase in base rates is probably unlikely. However, over the year, an upward move in defence of sterling and to curtail excess demand is probably inevitable.

Key

For the interim, the positive trade news may help to lengthen the horizon for dollar stability. Longer term, however, the markets could remain extremely wary of the dollar's vulnerability with the realized correction to the trade deficit falling far short of present expectations.

It is possible that with data releases not providing a clear direction of economic activity, monetary policy could remain broadly unchanged. Short-term, dollar stability may provide a shift in policy emphasis to maintain sufficient growth momentum for the election year ahead, which could allow a slight softening in rates. However, the huge funding requirement and need to retain interest in dollar denominated assets should preclude any significant downward adjustment. Longer term, with further dollar weakness anticipated, upward pressure on rates might resume.

Despite Bank of England calls for a prudent UK budget, the Chancellor's commitment to tax cuts suggests that interest rates could remain the dominant vehicle to implement restraint. In the run-up to the budget an imminent increase in base rates is probably unlikely. However, over the year, an upward move in defence of sterling and to curtail excess demand is probably inevitable.

Summary

On occasions the tone of your documents can be as crucial as the information content in terms of achieving the desired reaction from your reader. It is not so much *what* is written but *how* it is written which can affect the reader one way or another. When a vital sales contract or a personal career-linked recommendation is at issue, linguistic proficiency is as important as information precision.

The three language devices that regulate the tone of a document are:
- the use of a particular type of verb referred to as a modal
- the use, or not, of certain introductory phrases
- the selection of vocabulary that carries particular semantic nuances.

7 Developing a business style

The most crucial aspect in the writing of documents which are geared to project a professional impact on the reader is the point of style. Here you will be given eight very practical and effective guidelines on how a formal, impersonal and official style can be produced. All the guidelines are linguistic in nature and very effective in practice.

When reporting in a commercial setting the style of your writing is a crucial element in the effectiveness of the document. Too much emphasis and focus on either yourself or the reader should be avoided. After all, the central issue, the problem, the machine, the process, the policy or whatever is the subject matter of the document should receive priority over any other aspect, especially personal aspects.

The written message

In order to develop a style which projects an impersonal image we should acknowledge the distinction between speaking and writing: they are two completely distinct disciplines. An uncontrolled lapse into the more natural speech habit can mar the effectiveness of the written message.

Compare these two extremes of style and indicate which one you think is the more acceptable *written* style.

1 A The purpose of this report is to inform management of the status of the contextual analysis problem experienced with components supplied by Integrated Automation.

1 B What I want this report to do is to let management know about the present and current situation of the contextual analysis problem which we are experiencing with the components which as you know are supplied by Integrated Automation.

2 A   What you've got to do is to enter the code which you want from the ones that you see on the list on the VDU.

2 B   Enter the required code from those presented on the menu.

3 A   If more programmes are to be transferred the process described in points 7 to 12 should be repeated.

3 B   If you've to get more programmes transferred then what I'd suggest you do is what I've already told you in points 7 thru to 12; just do exactly the same thing.

4 A   The inspectors were given ample time at the beginning of the test to become familiar with the operation of the bar-code reader equipment.

4 B   Those people who came to inspect were given quite enough time right at the beginning of the test to know exactly everything about the operation of the bar-code reader equipment.

5 A   This description of the steps to be taken is really for people to use who are members of the Data Centre and are in charge of, and been given permission to do, this type of transfer.

5 B   This procedure is intended for use by members of the Data Centre responsible and authorized to carry out such transfers.

6 A   It is recommended that all personnel are informed immediately of these changes.

6 B   I think personnel should be told now about the changes we have made.

If your answers are A B A A B A, then you have a sound idea of the style required for commercial documents.

Case study

Masayuki Arisaka is a computer operator at a chemical processing plant in Scotland. He has been working there for six months after receiving an intensive English language course and a crash course on computer operations in the local refinery near Tokyo.

One day, unknown to Masayuki, he had computed incorrect data. This resulted in a heavy chemical loss due to water flooding in the chemical-package-drainage-system. As this proved very costly to the company, an enquiry was set up to ascertain the cause of this accident. Of course, a report on this enquiry was duly written. Below are two versions of the concluding parts of the report. Which style do you prefer?

Version 1

Conclusions and Recommendations

I don't think this accident was the fault of Mr
Arisaka. It was really the company's fault. They
didn't provide enough supervisors or good enough
training for their operators, and we'll probably
have quite a few more accidents like this if we
don't do something about it. What I suggest is that
we put on some sort of English language course. We
could test all the operators' English before they
start their computer training, so that we're sure
that they know enough English to understand what
they're told. Those that aren't good enough could
have some special training. It would be a good idea
to employ more supervisors in the computer room too.
If we do that there would always be enough of them
to supervise all the big operations that take place
there.

Version 2

Conclusions and Recommendations

It would seem clear from the evidence presented at
the enquiry that the accident was not caused by
negligence on the part of Mr Arisaka. On the
contrary, the company's failure to provide adequate
training and supervision for its operators seems to
have been the principal cause. Clearly, further
accidents of this nature must be expected if the
situation is not rectified, and the following action
is therefore recommended:

1. Provision should be made for all operators to
   undergo English language assessment prior to
   their period of computer training. This would
   ensure that their English was of a sufficiently
   high standard to follow the instruction.

> 2. The number of supervisors working in the computer
> room should be increased to ensure that there
> is sufficient staff to supervise all major
> operations.

Version 1 is written in a style that you might expect of an oral rather than a written presentation. Version 2 is a more impersonal, formal written style that is more acceptable for reports and memos. The differences in the two styles have a language base. A comparative analysis of these extremes reveals that if you wish to develop an acceptable written style you should:

avoid
- personal pronouns: *I, we*, etc.
- contractions: *don't, we're, I'd*, etc.
- repetition of words and/or meaning
- lengthy sentences

and **write**
- sentences with the *issue under focus* placed at the beginning *not* buried in the middle;
- opinions expressed using an 'it' construction or even using the imperative as when issuing orders;
- words that are clearly part of *written* and not *spoken* discourse;
- sentences that are *clearly* and *logically* linked.

If you are sensitive to these eight aspects of style you will be amazed at the difference in your own writing style. These changes can transform an amateur document into a very acceptable piece of discourse. To verify this you should work through the next two case studies. The initial exercise will give you an idea of how effective a text can be if it is in alignment with the points suggested. Afterwards give yourself an opportunity to attempt the transformation yourself. After a comparison of your version with the model offered you will be given a further chance to exercise your skills of applying formal written techniques to your writing tasks.

The case of Judith Harland

Judith Harland is an accommodation officer for a construction company in Caracas, Venezuela. One day she wrote to her boss.

To: Juan Vassini

From: Judith Harland   Date: October 6, 19__

Subject: TAQAIMANO AND BRENCO BEACH VILLAS

SECTION 1
I understand when I went on my vacation that you
were going to inspect these villas with a view to
looking at the complaints we have received from
employees and ways of solving them.

SECTION 2
I think it is fair to say that the Taqaimano
villas have had far more breakdowns in electrical
and plumbing apparatus than the Brenco Beach
villas. Both groups of villas are being serviced
by the builders for the first year. The Taqaimano
contractors are very slow to react and bad
workers. The Brenco Beach contractors are much
better and emergency a/c and plumbing problems are
taken up on the first day as a rule providing it
isn't a weekend.

SECTION 3
I have made an agreement with Brenco that any jobs
our employees required (which are normally handled
by our own crews on the other villas) should be
handled by Brenco's maintenance crews on a work
order basis and we would eventually receive an
invoice. Unfortunately, I understand that Brenco's
maintenance crews are not used to the sort of work
our people require (i.e. putting up pictures is a
typical example) and their work is not as good.
Brenco's maintenance crews will undertake any
requested work but it takes days to happen.
Furthermore, our employees have all heard about
the reputation of our own maintenance crew and
they cannot understand why they can't use the same
facilities. As far as I'm aware the following
items still need solving.

<u>Taqaimano Villas</u>

SECTION 4

A/C in kitchen and laundry. Maintenance have looked at this already and come up with a list of suggestions to improve it. Unfortunately Brenco would not fit an exhaust fan in the kitchen but agreed to fit an extractor fan over the cookers.

We have actually built and fitted a door between laundry room and kitchen and I am advised that the a/c is now much better.

I suspect that the utility room needs to be rearranged. The dryer is taking up too much space. A free standing shelf unit is also required for storage purposes.

<u>Brenco Beach Villas</u>

SECTION 5

There are a number of small items which require attention, i.e. replacement toilet seats, fitting of bolts and door handles, altering springs on gates.

I accept what Bill Smith says about door handles but the main contractors after arriving with a totally different colour now say they can't find any of the original colour - so what am I to do? Maybe we can back-charge Brenco.

I would urge that our own maintenance crew handle all but the major utility breakdowns in these villas and at least give our employees the same service as the rest of them.

This inter-office communication can be criticized on several issues pertaining to information control, language control and presentation techniques. We will deal first with *language control* and *style* in particular.

Let us analyse each section of Judith's report. The report has been broken into sections for ease of reference during our analysis.

Section 1

I understand when I went on my vacation that you were going to inspect these villas with a view to looking at the complaints we have received from employees and ways of solving them.

This sentence is too long. Judith has consequently made matters difficult both for herself and the reader. Grammatical mistakes often occur when a writer uses long sentences. Furthermore, pronouns may be difficult to identify. For example, the last word 'them' could grammatically refer back to either *complaints* or *employees*. Common sense is activated to guide the reading task and reference to *complaints* becomes obvious. Such an added cognitive task only hinders the reader.

Alternative version

It is understood that during my vacation these villas were to be inspected. This was scheduled to:
- assess employee complaints
- resolve any problems.

Four main features of style surface here:

1. There are no personal pronouns.
2. Sentences are short and clear.
3. The two sentences have been linked by using 'This' to refer back to a previous idea. This linking technique is considered in Chapter 9.
4. Dependent phrases have been cosmetically highlighted in the presentation of the second sentence. Each has a separate line and a bullet point. You will consider this in more detail in Chapter 8.

Section 2

I think it is fair to say that the Taqaimano villas have had far more breakdowns in electrical and plumbing apparatus than the Brenco Beach villas. Both groups of villas are being serviced by the builders for the first year. The Taqaimano contractors are very slow to react and bad workers. The Brenco Beach contractors are much better and emergency a/c and plumbing problems are taken up on the first day as a rule providing it isn't a weekend.

I think it is fair to say is undoubtedly a speech phrase. Using such words in the written text is a common tendency. A little thought would produce a far more acceptable written style. In this case the word *Certainly* would suffice.

In speech we often use words that are technically or semantically incorrect. This practice is sometimes acceptable as in:

The machine can't do its job properly.

The kettle is boiling its head off.

Generally, the practice is considered unacceptable, as in:

The Taqaimano villas have had far more breakdowns ...

Villas do not break down—machines do.

Again, in speech we often do not use grammatically correct sentence structures. In writing this is completely unacceptable. Consider:

The Taqaimano contractors are very slow to react and bad workers.

The grammatical scope of the word *are* will cover *very slow to react* but not *bad workers* in the same sentence. The reason for this is that these units of words do not have the same balance; therefore *and* will not join them. If you change *bad workers* to *very quick to complain*, the sentence is grammatically correct.

The Taqaimano contractors are very slow to react and very quick to complain.

A similar tendency has been used in the final sentence of this section—*providing it isn't a weekend.* But here also Judith has used a contraction, *isn't*, a practice which emphasizes the spoken style.

Alternative version

The builders are servicing both groups of villas for the first year. Certainly, more electrical and plumbing breakdowns have occurred at the Taqaimano villas. This could be due to the fact that the contractors are slow to react. Furthermore, their work is below standard.

In contrast, the Brenco contractors:
- work efficiently and
- react to emergency calls promptly.

Two main features of style surface here.

1. Each sentence is clearly linked to the one before.
2. The dependent clauses in the last paragraph have been cosmetically highlighted by giving each a separate line and a bullet point.

Section 3

I have made an agreement with Brenco that any jobs our employees required (which are normally handled by our own crews on the other villas) should be handled by Brenco's maintenance crews on a work order basis and we would eventually receive an invoice. Unfortunately, I understand that Brenco's maintenance crews are not used to the sort of work our people require (i.e. putting up pictures is a typical example) and their work is not as good. Brenco's maintenance crews will undertake any requested work but it takes days to happen. Furthermore, our employees have all heard about the reputation of our own maintenance crew and they can't understand why they can't use the same facilities. As far as I'm aware the following items still need solving.

Judith here continues in the same style:

- There is frequent repetition of *maintenance crews.*
- We encounter the personal pronoun *I* at the beginning of the paragraph.
- Too many ideas are haphazardly connected by *and.*
- Three times we find contractions in the last two sentences—*can't* and *I'm.*
- Too many sentences begin with an active issue instead of the passive issue under focus, thus losing emphasis.

> *I have made an agreement with Brenco ...*
> [should be written]
> *An agreement has been made with Brenco ...*
>
> *... we would eventually receive an invoice ...*
> [should be written]
> *... an invoice would eventually be received.*
>
> *Our employees have all heard about the reputation of our own maintenance crew.*
> [should be written]
> *The reputation of our own maintenance crew is well known.*
>
> *They can't understand why they can't use the same facilities.*
> [should be written]
> *It is not understood why the same facilities cannot be used.*

- Speech phrases saturate the entire extract, e.g. *it takes days to happen.*

It is better to use:

now	rather than	*at this point in time*
approximately	rather than	*at about*
prior to	rather than	*before that time*
many/much	rather than	*a lot of*
prove to be uneconomical	rather than	*is going to cost too much*
approval	rather than	*go-ahead*
residual	rather than	*left over*

Alternative version

An agreement has been made with Brenco to deal with our employees' requirements. This will be on a work order basis for which an invoice would be raised.

Our own maintenance group is far superior to Brenco's crew. Consequently, it is not understood why the same facilities cannot be used to maintain the Brenco villas.

Two main features of style emerge here.

1. The use of the passive voice at the beginning of sentences (e.g. *An agreement has been made* ...).
2. The avoidance of speech patterns in words and phrases.

Keeping in mind the eight aspects of an acceptable written style, rewrite sections 4 and 5; then compare your versions with those below.

Section 4

```
Taqaimano Villas

Our maintenance group has looked at the
air-conditioning units in the kitchen and laundry.
Brenco has now agreed to fit an extractor fan over
the cookers.

A door has been fitted between the laundry room and
the kitchen. It is understood that the
air-conditioning is now much better.

The utility room needs to be rearranged. The dryer
is taking up too much space. A free standing shelf
is required so that:

- the dryer can be placed on a shelf.
- further storage space is made available.
```

Section 5

Brenco Beach Villas

Here a number of small items require maintenance:

- replacing toilet seats
- fitting bolts and door handles
- adjusting springs on gates

Door handles of a similar colour to the originals must be found.

Recommendations

All major utility breakdowns should be handled by the contractors.

Other maintenance work should be undertaken by our own crews.

Case study

Now let us examine further some of the points regarding a formal written style by studying the case of Kurt Forester.

Kurt is the personnel manager of a large multinational in Brussels. He has recently been plagued by requests from the heads of various divisions to upgrade certain employees. However, the economic climate over the last few years has tightened the promotion belt, thus causing motivational problems for department heads who have to find ways of rewarding high flyers.

The following are two versions of a report Kurt wrote to the deputy managing director of finance and administration.

Version 1

From: Personnel Manager   Date: 7.12.19__

To: DMD, Finance and
           Administration   Ref: DMD/FIN/278

Subject: Request for Promotion on Exceptional Basis

I wish to draw your attention to the fact that we
have received recommendations for exceptional
up-gradings from Department Heads. These have
increased significantly during the past year. If we
complied with these recommendations, we would in
fact distort the principle of Job Evaluation applied
throughout the Company and also create
dissatisfaction among other employees.

However, we realize that there could be a certain
procedure drawn up to compensate these employees who
are potentially competent, but blocked by the
existing restrictions.

In this connection, we suggest to establish a set of
rules which would provide a flexibility and
consistency in treating such exceptional
up-gradings, and at the same time would prevent a
relaxation of the standard policy.

After reviewing the recommendations received, we
believe that we should only consider employees
classified at grade 10 and above, who meet one of
the following criteria:

a. Those who are filling a higher job in an acting
capacity for at least one year due to the
secondment or some other reason for
non-availability of the incumbent.
b. Those who have reached the ceiling of their
grades and have not been granted an increase on
their salaries for at least two years.

I would like you to endorse these suggestions if
they meet your approval as soon as possible.

Version 2

From: Personnel Manager   Date: 7.12.19--

To: DMD, Finance and
         Administration   Ref: DMD/FIN/278

Subject:<u>Request for Promotion on Exceptional Basis</u>

Recommendations for exceptional up-gradings have been received from Department Heads. These have increased significantly during the past year. The principle of Job Evaluation applied throughout the Company would be distorted if approval were given to these recommendations. In addition, employee dissatisfaction would be created.

However, a certain procedure could be drawn up in order to compensate employees who are potentially competent, but blocked by the existing restrictions.

In this connection, a set of rules should be established which would provide flexibility and consistency in treating such exceptional up-gradings and at the same time would prevent a relaxation of the standard policy.

On reviewing the recommendations received, it is felt that consideration should only be given to employees classified at grade 10 and above who meet one of the following criteria:

a. Those who are filling a higher job in an acting capacity for at least one year due to the secondment or some other reason for non-availability of the incumbent.

b. Those who have reached the ceiling of their grades and have not been granted an increase on their salaries for at least two years.

Your early approval of these suggestions would be appreciated.

Now assess the following statements on two very important aspects of style: use of personal pronouns and the formation of sentences.

Personal pronouns

		True	False
1	Version 1 uses personal pronouns which direct the reader's attention away from the issue under focus and onto the writer.	[T]	[F]
2	Such a practice helps the writer to achieve his objective.	[T]	[F]
3	Version 2 does not use any personal pronouns yet imparts the same factual information as the first version.	[T]	[F]
4	In the last sentence of version 2, Kurt expresses an opinion without using *I*.	[T]	[F]
5	Such a practice helps the writer to achieve his objective by focusing the reader's attention on the issue at hand.	[T]	[F]

Sentence structure

6	Topics such as issues, problems, machinery, schedules, policies, processes, etc., are nouns of a passive rather than an active nature.	[T]	[F]
7	When this noun is a key topic, burying it in the middle of a sentence helps the reader to keep 'on track'.	[T]	[F]
8	The following sentences begin with an active topic:	[T]	[F]
	• The message was transmitted yesterday.		
	• The savings of members would be efficiently managed.	[T]	[F]

	True	False
• The deficit can be easily explained.	[T]	[F]
• The concept of index funds was initially dismissed.	[T]	[F]
• A review of the role of the societies was promised in April.	[T]	[F]
• No definite objectives have yet been made explicit.	[T]	[F]

9 The following sentences begin with a passive topic: [T]   [F]
  • I have planned a timetable for review.
  • Brokers forecast a 15 per cent increase over the next six months.   [T]   [F]
  • The analysts pinpoint the stock market crash as the cause of the slowdown in trade.   [T]   [F]
  • I cannot recommend any further investment in the project.   [T]   [F]
  • The engineers suggest an immediate overhaul of the existing structure.   [T]   [F]
  • I last reviewed the situation on 16 May when the shares were 604p.   [T]   [F]

Answers   1T 2F 3T 4T 5T 6T 7F 8 all F 9 all F

10 A final exercise on writing sentences in the passive voice—rewrite the sentences in (9) beginning each with the central issue. Do not change the meaning. Afterwards compare your version with the model sentences below.
  • A timetable has been planned for review.
  • A 15 per cent increase is forecast over the next six months.
  • The slowdown in trade is attributed to the stock market crash.
  • Further investment in the project cannot be recommended.
  • An immediate overhaul of the existing structure is suggested.
  • The situation was last reviewed on 16 May when the shares were 604p.

Expressing opinions

One of the most crucial sections of a report is where facts and interpretations are processed by the writer and expressed as personal/professional opinions. It is advisable (if you want to project a professional image) that these opinions are expressed in a style that observes the eight considerations discussed in this chapter.

Review the alternative styles presented below, remembering that here the sentences have been taken out of context. Nevertheless, the reader would still be aware of who is expressing these opinions: the writer's name would be at the top and invariably his or her signature would be penned at the end of the document.

Circle (a) or (b) to indicate the better formal style.

1.a   I suggest selling these shares now.
1.b   Sell these shares now.

2.a   I expect to see steady accumulation by institutional investors.
2.b   A steady accumulation by institutional investors is expected.

3.a   I do not anticipate any threat of a fall before November.
3.b   A threat of a fall before November is not anticipated.

4.a   I think that investors should stay wary of the problems in the economy.
4.b   Investors should stay wary of the problems in the economy.

5.a   I believe that the demand situation should favour higher share prices.
5.b   The demand situation should favour higher share prices.

6.a   It is recommended that a fundamental change in advertising policy is confirmed before the launch.
6.b   I think that we should confirm a fundamental change in advertising policy before the launch.

7.a   I think that shares have little to recommend them.
7.b   Shares have little to recommend them.

8.a   I think that we should increase capital spending.
8.b   Increase capital spending.

9.a   I would like to recommend that we send a letter of rejection to Davenport Industries.
9.b   Send a letter of rejection to Davenport Industries.

10.a   Wisely Arrow appears to prove that British textile companies really can prosper in the current tough conditions.

10.b   I think that Wisely Arrow appears to prove that British textile companies really can prosper in the current tough conditions.

Suggested options: 1.b, 2.b, 3.b, 4.b, 5.b, 6.a, 7.b, 8.b, 9.b, 10.a

Recommendations

A recommendation is a professionally 'thought out' opinion supported by an expressed conclusion. Linguistically, there are several formats which can be adopted. Here is the same recommendation in four different formats.

1   Investigate apparent problems in perforator performance.
2   The apparent problems in perforator performance should be investigated.
3   There is a need to investigate the apparent problems in perforator performance.
4   I think that we should investigate the apparent problems in perforator performance.

The format used in most reports is number 1. This is clear and concise and, in some companies, standard practice. Which of the opinions in the previous exercise uses this style?

Answers: 1.b, 8.b, 9.b

Speech patterns

The style of a report is often marred by the invasion of speech patterns, especially repetition, tautology and circumlocution.

Repetition, where the same word is used needlessly more than once, is a common weakness in commercial documents.

e.g.   *Many operators think that operators have nothing better to do than operate.*

A more notable weakness is where the same concept is repeated. We call this **tautology**.

e.g.   *I would like to buy a hot water heater.*
        Could you reverse back a little?

Circumlocution, where a concept is expressed in more words than necessary, is the third weakness. It is not exactly repetition but, like repetition and tautology, it can be classed as employing superfluous words.

e.g.　*Everyone realizes that his statements conform little to the reality of the precise situation in question.*

The cause of these aberrations from the norm in formal written documents is most definitely an invasion of speech habits. When we are talking we tend to repeat words or their meaning with little respect for the exactness expected of the written dissertation. Furthermore, to ensure our contributions to a conversation *sound* fluent, potential vacuums are very often filled with unnecessary words; these may be very important when engaged in a two-way *oral* communication process. In writing, however, you must be concise, exact and to the point. Compare the following two versions of the same report.

```
An Analysis of the Sales-Related Problems Facing
Futuristic Design, Inc.

1.0 Summary

    From the outset and since its establishment in
    1978 Futuristic Design, Inc. has been operating
    at almost near to maximum capacity. This has
    resulted in the annual average sales of
    approximately $3m for each year. In September
    1989, the President of Futuristic Design Inc.,
    Mr Vagn Andersen requested that there should be
    a 20% increase in production and sales.

    This increase was requested in order to maximize
    the effort of generating more profit which would
    result as a consequence to the increase in
    production.

    As a result of this request by the President, Mr
    Andersen, management decided to make some
    changes and alterations in the organizational
    structure of the company to facilitate and
    expedite this increase in production. These
    modifications were primarily decided upon to
```

ensure that the increase in sales would not be impeded by an inability to increase production.

However, the proposed increase in production and the modifications proposed in the organizational structure led to the resignation of two senior members of the company. These personnel were in high positions and felt forced to resign as a result of the changes referred to above.

Three months following the implementation of the new organizational structure of the company, it was obvious to all concerned and so became apparent that there was an adverse effect to the implementation of these policies. In brief, to sum up, there had been a continuous decline in the company's sales. This downturn in trade was attributed to the poor quality of the products and the outdated design of the products.

An initial and preliminary investigation at the outset revealed and showed that the high production quotas and the changes in the organizational structure led to a deterioration in the communicative links between subordinates and supervisors. This, it was thought, in turn, led to the creation of a poor and ineffective working environment throughout the workplace in the company.

After a thorough and detailed investigation of the issues which were causing the problems which began to be experienced by the employees, we would like to recommend that management should set up, establish and implement a clearly defined set of policies and procedures with regard to the chain of command, disciplinary measures, promotion and recruitment. Furthermore, and in addition to these recommendations, we recommend the setting up and establishment of quality circles and the introduction of a training scheme for both managers and supervisors.

Before you read the more acceptable text below, you may like to write your own version so that you can compare notes.

An Analysis of the Sales-Related Problems Facing Futuristic Design, Inc.

Summary

Since its establishment in 1978, Futuristic Design, Inc. has been operating at approximately maximum capacity resulting in average annual sales of nearly $3m.

In September 1989 the President, Mr Vagn Andersen, requested a 20% increase in production and sales in an effort to generate more profit. Following this request management decided on certain alterations in the organizational structure to facilitate the increase in production. These changes led to the resignation of two senior members of management.

Three months following the implementation of the new policies, it became apparent that poor quality and outdated design of products were, in effect, contributing to a decline in sales. Preliminary investigations revealed that high production quotas and sudden changes in organizational structure led to a breakdown in communication between subordinates and supervisors. This, in turn, created a poor working environment.

After a thorough investigation the following recommendations are made:

1. Management should establish and implement clearly defined policies and procedures regarding:
   - chain of command
   - disciplinary measures
   - promotion
   - recruitment
2. Quality control procedures should be proposed, including training programmes for both management and supervisors.

Review exercises

Exercise one

Do the following sentences begin with a passive issue?

	Yes	No
1 John Shaklee checks the accounts every month.	[Y]	[N]
2 The plant supervisor reviews the schedules on a daily basis.	[Y]	[N]
3 The maintenance engineer has coated the pipeline.	[Y]	[N]
4 She had written her report before the supervisor presented her with the new evidence.	[Y]	[N]
5 I last reviewed the shares in July 1989.	[Y]	[N]
6 We have never really required this massive storage capacity.	[Y]	[N]

The answer to all these is *No*. Now, unless the person is the key component of the writer's message, these sentences can all be framed in a more impersonal and, therefore, more acceptable commercial written style.

Keeping the same meaning, try to construct these sentences without referring to the person. Of course, in your own written documents, if the person is also important then obviously he or she must be mentioned. In the first example, if it is important for the reader to know that it is John Shaklee and not Bill Baker who checks the accounts every month, then he must be mentioned. Invariably, however, it is the accounts which the writer will be focusing on, so the sentence should read:

1   The accounts are checked every month.

Now you complete the following sentences.

2   The schedules . . .

_____

3   The pipeline . . .

_____

4   The report ...

_____

5   The shares ...

_____

6   This massive storage capacity ...

_____

_____

Suggested answers:
2   The schedules are reviewed daily.
3   The pipeline has been coated.
4   The report had been written before the new evidence had been presented by the supervisor.
5   The shares were last reviewed in July 1989.
6   This massive storage capacity has never really been required.

Exercise two

Rewrite the following text, highlighting the passive issues underlined.

The manager's secretary arranged <u>a meeting</u> between Mr Shipley and the representative of the contractors. They discussed <u>the completion date</u> of the new refinery, and they reached <u>an agreement</u> that commissioning would begin on 10 April 1992. The contractor will pay compensation to <u>the company</u> for late completion but the company will pay a bonus to <u>the contractor</u> for completion before 10 April 1992. They arranged <u>another meeting</u> for the following week at which they would sign <u>the contracts</u>.

Now compare your version with the following:

A meeting was arranged between Mr Shipley, the representative of the contractors. The completion date of the new refinery was discussed and an agreement was reached that commissioning would begin on 10 April 1992. Compensation will be paid to the company for late completion but a bonus will be paid to the contractor for completion before 10 April 1992. Another meeting was arranged for the following week at which the contracts would be signed.

Exercise three

Read the following memo.

To: Production Manager

From: Production Engineer

Date: January 11, 19___

Subject: <u>Evaluation of Bids for Video Chart Reader</u>

I'd like to recommend that we send a letter of
rejection to Copis for the above mentioned project
and that we send a letter of agreement to Tamco for
their bid. I'm preparing the letter of agreement and
I'll send it to you when it's ready for your
agreement.

<u>Evaluation</u>

We have decided to decide on Tamco instead of Copis
because they can get the goods sent in a shorter
time. I think that both contractors have high prices
for the spinal portion of the bid. I'm sure this
will more than likely be negotiable at that time.
The Copis bid includes a printer and a plotter which
we did not ask for and both the printer and the
plotter are not really up to what we require.

The following breaks down the bids by Company and
requested bid items.

Bid Form Item	Tamco	Copis
1. Delivery Time	28 days	60 days
2. 6 Month Lease	US$ 2300.00/MO	US$ 2200.00/MO
3. Optional 1 yr Lease	US$ 750.00/MO	US$ 1100.00/MO
4. Software Options		
Data Printout	yes	yes
Calibration Printout	yes	yes
Cartesian Plot	yes	yes
Log-Log Plot	yes	yes
Semilog Plot	yes	yes

We expect this instrumentation to make better the
reliability of the flowing survey data used in gas
lift analysis. The data we acquire from using this

package will be compared with downhole electronic
recording data and we will be able to determine
which instrumentation needs we will need to include
in future wireline contracts.

Now rewrite the memo in a more formal written style and then
compare with the version below.

To: Production Manager   Ref: 71RFPT

From: Production Engineer   Date: January 11, 19__

Subject: Request for Purchase Approval of Video
          Chart Reader

1.0 Recommendation

    After careful evaluation it is recommended that
    Tamco's Video Chart Reader should be considered
    for purchase.

2.0 Bid Form Items Breakdown

    2.1 Lease Rates in US Dollars Per Month

Duration	Copis	Tamco
6 months	2200.00	2300.00
1 year (Optional)	1100.00	750.00

    2.2 Delivery Time

    Copis 60 days
    Tamco 28 days

    2.3 Software Options

    Both Tamco and Copis support the following
    options:

    2.3.1 Data Printout
    2.3.2 Calibration Printout
    2.3.3 Cartesian Plot
    2.3.4 Log-Log Plot
    2.3.5 Semilog Plot

3.0 <u>Justification</u>

The acquisition of this package will improve the
reliability of the flowing survey data in gas
lift analysis. This data can then be compared
with data downhole which is electronically
recorded. This will help in determining which
instrumentation needs to be included in future
wireline contracts.

Summary

In this chapter the two disciplines of speaking and writing have been
compared. It is obvious that the more spontaneous and more frequently
used patterns of speech will inevitably interfere with your task of
achieving a formal written style for commercial documentation. To keep
this interference to a minimum, eight practices—four to avoid and four
to use—have been proposed.

Avoid
- personal pronouns
- contractions
- long sentences
- repetition of words and/or meanings

Use
- passive voice structure
- impersonal 'it' constructions
- formal (yet simple) vocabulary
- clear linking techniques (see Chapter 9).

8 Making a document attractive

It is surprising that the least difficult yet most effective techniques for creating that SOLDIER image are fundamentally cosmetic. Before the first cursory glance through a text, a reader subconsciously responds to the attractiveness of the paper. Some people can be seduced by the appearance of a car or a piece of furniture. Once drawn by the contours, colour and texture, the functional use is examined. So too with your documents. If you have effectively controlled the content and language, then it would be irresponsible not to apply those presentation techniques which prompt the initial impact. These devices can be either visual or linguistic and have two crucial purposes: to make the document attractive and also to facilitate access to different parts of the text. The emphasis when considering presentation techniques is to make your document reader friendly.

Presentation techniques

With presentation techniques in mind, read the following document. It should take no longer than 20 seconds to assimilate the essential information.

```
This report deals with various methods of clearing
oil spills at sea for the purpose of recommending
the most effective method to be used by this
Company. Attempts have been made to burn oil.
Although wicking materials have been used to sustain
burning on the sea, they have not been completely
successful. It is not possible to burn oil on the
beach without special equipment. Burning may be
useful as a tool for dealing with fresh oil that
comes ashore or in sheltered waters close to the
shore. It is not an effective method for disposing
```

of spilt oil. Sinking agents are used to sink oil by
distributing a fine powder over the oil to increase
its density. This is a difficult operation and it
has been found that the sunken oil reaches the sea
bed in a form that might well contaminate fishing
gear and be detrimental to bottom flora and fauna.
Nevertheless, the method can be improved by treating
sand with amine to make it oleophilic, and applying
it as a sand/water slurry. Both methods are
effective, but have disadvantages, and therefore
should be used in emergency only. Booms may be used
to prevent the spread of oil over a wide area in the
open sea or in calm water. There are three methods
of using the booms: first towed by a suitable tug,
second moored in shallow water and third free
floating. However, oil escapes from underneath booms.
Moreover, they cannot be used in rough conditions.
Although booms have proved useful in containing oil
for recovery, they are not 100% effective.
Dispersants are chemicals used for breaking up spilt
oil at sea and these have been found to be the most
satisfactory method of attack. Achieving the best
results with dispersant chemicals depends upon two
factors: first, the distribution of the appropriate
amount of the chemical over the floating oil, and
secondly, the mixing or agitation of the treated oil
with the upper layer of the sea. Equipment which has
proved highly successful in performing the mixing
requirement is available and can be fitted to any
tug. Despite the huge quantity used to break up the
floating oil, it causes negligible harm to marine
life. An in-depth study revealed that using
dispersants is the most effective method. Dispersant
chemicals should be introduced to the department and
adequate quantity stored in case of oil spills in
this area. One of the most efficient and least toxic
of this new family of dispersants is produced under
the trade name BP 1100X, and it is recommended that
an order for this should be placed with the
manufacturers immediately.

Now perform the same reading task on this document. Once again, 20 seconds should be enough time to assimilate the essential information.

METHODS OF CLEARING OIL SPILLS AT SEA

1.0 Purpose

This report deals with various methods of clearing oil spills at sea for the purpose of recommending the most effective method to be used by this company.

2.0 Scope

Four methods have been studied. These are treated separately in Section 3 (3.1 – 3.4).

Conclusions and recommendations are to be found in Sections 4 and 5 respectively.

3.0 Techniques

3.1 Burning

Attempts have been made to burn oil. Although wicking materials have been used to sustain burning on the sea, they have not been completely successful. It is not possible to burn oil on the beach without special equipment. Burning may be useful as a tool for dealing with fresh oil that comes ashore or in sheltered waters close to the shore. It is not an effective method for disposing of spilt oil.

3.2 Sinking

Sinking agents are used to sink oil by distributing a fine powder over the oil to increase its density. This is a difficult operation and it has been found that the sunken oil reaches the sea bed in a form that might well contaminate fishing gear and be detrimental to bottom flora and fauna. Nevertheless, the method can be improved by treating sand with amine to make it oleophilic, and applying it as a sand/water slurry. Both methods are effective, but have disadvantages, and therefore should only be used in emergency.

3.3 Booms

Booms may be used to prevent the spread of oil over a wide area in the open sea or in calm water. There are three methods of using the booms: first, towed by a suitable tug, second, moored in shallow water and, third, free floating. The problem with all of these is that oil escapes from underneath the boom. Moreover, they cannot be used in rough conditions. Although booms have proved useful in containing oil for recovery, they are not 100% effective.

3.4 Dispersants

Dispersants are chemicals used for breaking up spilt oil at sea and these have been found to be the most satisfactory method of attack. Achieving the best results with dispersant chemicals depends upon two factors: first, the distribution of an appropriate amount of the chemical over the floating oil and, secondly, the mixing or agitation of the treated oil with the upper layer of the sea. Equipment which has proved highly successful in performing the mixing requirement is available and can be fitted to any tug. Despite the huge quantity used to break up floating oil on the open sea, it causes negligible harm to marine life.

```
4.0 Conclusion

    By studying the four methods of dealing with oil
    spills at sea it was found that dispersant is
    the most effective method.

5.0 Recommendations

    Dispersant chemicals should be introduced to the
    department and adequate quantity stored in case
    of oil spills in this area. One of the most
    efficient and least toxic of this new family of
    dispersants is produced under the trade name BP
    1100X, and it is recommended that an order for
    this should be placed with the manufacturers
    immediately.
```

Of course, both reports are the same in terms of information and language control. The second version, however, is far easier to process, far more reader friendly. The difference is merely cosmetic; yet it is a vital ingredient in effective written documentation. The specific areas are:

1. Visual
   - space
   - indentation
   - numbering

2. Linguistic
   - Labelling
     - subject heading
     - subheadings
   - Paragraph structure

Obviously, space is important if the format and attractiveness are to be achieved. This factor, together with the second consideration, indentations, can make an appealing report out of something which would otherwise look dreadfully dull. Indentations can be used to show that the writer is now dealing with a subsection, if this is lettered or numbered it makes for ease of reference for the readers. Consider the following short report.

TO: Operations Manager   Date: 1 December 19___

FROM: Project Supervisor   Ref: MPD/D

SUBJECT: <u>Tripod Well Head Jacket Installation
          Contract</u>

This work was for procurement, fabrication and
installation of one tripod well head jacket, in the
Mahazimi field. This contract was part of approved
1988 flowline and well head jacket programme. The
contract was awarded to McFermot during June 1990.
The entire work was scheduled to be completed by end
of December 1990.

1. <u>Principal Considerations</u>

<u>Planning</u>

a. The project was completed in accordance with
   approved implementation plan.

b. As a result of good planning the jacket was
   installed ahead of schedule.

<u>Technical</u>

Fabrication and installation activities were
controlled by supervision/inspection teams.

a. Pile driving criteria/procedure have been
   investigated and reviewed.

b. Point (a) became an important issue because of
   previous installation experience in this
   field.

c. Jacket was installed up to McFermot
   specification.

<u>Financial</u>

a. There were no delays or downtime costs.

b. A two barge installation programme was
   negotiated at no cost to the Corporation. This

> was much less weather-dependent than the
> proposed one.
>
> c. The jacket was installed within the approved
>   budget and with savings of 8 days of weather
>   downtime.
>
> 2. <u>Conclusion</u>
>
> This project was completed with a high degree of
> professional competence by the project team.
>
> 3. <u>Recommendation</u>
>
> The Corporation should have no hesitation in
> considering this project team for future projects.

Another use of this technique of indentation is now commonly adopted at the sentence level. For example, where a group of words, phrases or even clauses are dependent on a single word, phrase or clause, this relationship is clearly marked. The outcome shows a radical influence on the reader's task of assimilation.

Consider each version, then decide on the one that makes the information more readily accessible.

1 a. The tool selected for a fishing attempt should be in a good condition and offer a real chance of success. It is also important that this tool is the strongest possible for the dimensional clearance available. Finally, the tool should be well designed and manufactured.

  b. It is important that any tool selected for a fishing attempt should:
  - be the strongest possible for the dimensional clearance available;
  - be well designed and manufactured;
  - be in good condition;
  - offer a real chance of success.

2 a. The contractor must submit and sign a report on the project before it becomes legally acceptable. Of course, this is also subject to our examination of the pipeline by the company representative.

  b. The project will only become legally acceptable after:
  - the pipeline has been examined by the company representative;

- a report signed by the contractor has been submitted to the company.

3 a.   Because it secures a reasonable agreement and will be completed by 31.12.19__, the project should be awarded to Emcorp. Furthermore, Petcor specifications are hereby complied with if Emcorp are given the project.

 b.   Emcorp should be awarded the project because it:
- secures a reasonable agreement;
- complies with Petcor specifications;
- will be completed by 31.12.19—.

4 a.   Once the agreement has been signed, the cash will be transferred to the UK account, any interest will accrue at 10 per cent and the capital may not be utilized until one year from the date of signing.

 b.   *Terms and Conditions*
On signing the agreement:
- the cash will be transferred to the UK account;
- interest will accrue at 10 per cent;
- the capital may not be utilized for one year.

5 a.   A report was written which contains all relevant information. It also specifies the action required. This report, which contains procedural instructions, was written after the meeting.

 b.   After the meeting a report was written which:
- contains all relevant information;
- specifies the action required;
- provides procedural instructions.

There is no doubt that the *b* versions do help the reader. When tested in terms of assessing ease of assimilation, texts using this technique are always favoured. However, feedback indicates that overuse can be distracting and an irritant. For this reason some readers prefer the *a* version.

As a writer, you should use common sense, coupled with knowledge of reader expectancies, likes and dislikes.

Numbers and letters

The history of the numbering or lettering of written documents is very interesting. We have the Arab numbering system to the base 10 as in 1, 2, 3, 4, etc. The Greeks, not to be outdone, gave us their lettering system, both large and small as in A, B, C, D and a,b,c,d, etc.

The Romans also contributed to the scheme by offering their numbering system in both large and small numbers I, II, III, IV and (i), (ii), (iii) and (iv), etc.

Access to so many demarcation systems has confused the discipline of commercial reporting—some writers use one method, some another and others a combination—sometimes consistently, other times inconsistently.

An American influence now often adopted has gone back to the Arabic system but with a few modifications. With this version we now have a system which is consistent, easy to follow, user friendly and informative for the reader.

Main sections are given full number status followed by .0 as:

1.0

2.0

3.0

4.0, etc.

Subsections are numbered after the first period or point as:

1.1

1.2

1.3

These are all subsections of 1.0.

The same logic applies to sub-subsections:

2.3.1

2.3.2

2.3.3

These are all subsections of 2.3.

The great advantage of this system is that it always—subconsciously—prepares your readers for possible subsections. For example, once readers have covered section 3.2.2 you have informed them of one of four possible subdivisions to follow, i.e.

3.2.2.1

3.2.3

3.3

4.0

There is a disadvantage with this system in terms of sub-subsubdivisions. It can be irksome to encounter 23.5.7.2. You should be realistic and adopt a system to suit your text length. Usually a subdivision after the third subsection may be able to take bullets rather than numbers as a comparison of the following examples indicates:

To: Technical Service Superintendent

From: Processing Engineering Section Head

Date: 29 April 19__

Subject: Evaluation of Amine Plate Heat
         Exchanger Chemical Cleaning

The plate heat exchanger (E-102) of unit 2 was
cleaned by using an in-house developed chemical
cleaning procedure. This operation was conducted
from 2 April to 5 April 19__ to enhance its
performance which in turn will improve energy
utilization efficiency.

1.0 Recommendations

   1.1 Conduct this chemical cleaning for all heat
       exchangers in the plant (Operation Section)

   1.2 Study the optimum frequency for chemical
       cleaning operation (Process Engineering)

   1.3 Approach the professional chemical cleaning
       companies to seek their advice on the
       following:

       − chemicals to be used
       − procedures to be adopted
       − chemical cleaning equipment to be
         incorporated.

To: Technical Service Superintendent

From: Processing Engineering Section Head

Date: 29 April 19___

Subject: <u>Evaluation of Amine Plate Heat
           Exchanger Chemical Cleaning</u>

The plate heat exchanger (E-102) of unit 2 was
cleaned by using an in-house developed chemical
cleaning procedure. This operation was conducted
from 2 April to 5 April 19___ to enhance its
performance which in turn will improve energy
utilization efficiency.

1.0 <u>Recommendations</u>

    1.1 Conduct this chemical cleaning for all heat
        exchangers in the plant (Operation Section)

    1.2 Study the optimum frequency for chemical
        cleaning operation (Process Engineering)

    1.3 Approach the professional chemical cleaning
        companies to seek their advice on the
        following:

        1.3.1 chemicals to be used
        1.3.2 procedures to be adopted
        1.3.3 chemical cleaning equipment to be
              incorporated.

One more piece of advice regarding this system: once you have
adopted it, readers will subconsciously use it to ease their task. Any
incursion of another system might mar the consistency of the document.
In very long reports this facility is a bonus to reader assimilation tasks.
For example, which would you prefer?

1   16.5
2   P.5
3   16.e
4   XVI(v)

For the fifth subsection of Section 16, it seems obvious that the first option is the easiest both to read and to write.

Of course, for small memos and reports a mixture of numbers and letters is not too overpowering if used consistently and intelligently, as in the following letter from the credit relations manager of the New Abu Dhabi Bank.

---

4 January 1993

The Sultan Trading Co. Ltd
P O Box 189
Abu Dhabi

For the attention of Mr B. Sultan, Finance Director

Dear Sir,

The New Abu Dhabi Bank is pleased to place at your disposal a facility of up to Dhs. 1,000,000 (one million UAE Dirhams) on the following terms and conditions:

1 Utilization

   The facility is available to place at your disposal the instruments detailed below, provided that the aggregate outstanding does not exceed Dhs. 1,000,000.

   a. Up to Dhs. 500,000 by way of overdraft

   b. Up to Dhs. 1,000,000 by way of eurocurrency advances

   c. Up to Dhs. 750,000 by way of letters of credit, the tenors of which shall not exceed one year.

2 Pricing

   a. Overdraft Interest

      Interest shall be payable on overdrafts at the rate of 1% per annum above the Bank's published base rate and shall be payable quarterly in arrears. Interest shall be calculated on a 360-day year basis.

b. Loan Interest

Interest shall be payable on advances at 1/4% per annum above the London Inter Bank Offer Rate and shall be payable on the maturity of each advance. Interest shall be calculated on a 360-day year basis.

3 Commissions and Fees

a. Letter of Credit Commissions

Commission will be charged on letters of credit at the following rates:

Up to Dhs. 10,000 — 2% (minimum charge of Dhs. 5) Dhs. 10,001 — Dhs 100,000 — 0.5% Dhs. 100,001 — Dhs. 1,000,000 — 0.40%.

b. Commitment Fee

A commitment fee of 1/4% per annum will be charged on the unused amount of the facility.

4 Conditions

a. This facility will remain in operation at all times subject to your company maintaining the following financial covenants:

— Net worth greater than Dhs. 4,000,000
— Debt/Net worth less than 2.0:1
— Current Ratio greater than 1.5:1

as certified by your auditors.

b. You will be required to submit your audited financial statements within 90 days of your financial year end.

c. There will be no change of ownership without the Bank's prior written consent.

d. The Bank will remain 'pari passu' with all of her lenders to you.

5 <u>Expiry</u>

This facility will, subject to the conditions above, remain in operation until 31 January 1994. Whilst it may be our intention to renew the facility at that date, we reserve the right to be repaid for all outstandings under this line as they fall due.

This offer is open for acceptance until 28 February 1993 at which time, if not accepted, the offer will lapse. To signify acceptance of this facility please sign the attached duplicate of this letter and return to the Bank together with:

a. The Articles of Association of the Company.

b. A board resolution authorizing the acceptance of the facility and the signatories to operate the line.

c. Specimen signatures of the above signatories.

We look forward to receiving the above documents at the start of our business relationship.

Yours faithfully,

Credit Relations Manager

Labels

A method of instruction used in public places, like supermarkets and airports, is the use of signposts. The more specific they are the more helpful they are to the public. The same maxim applies if your endeavours are focused on making things easy for your readers. These signposts are labels which prepare the readers for what follows. Any deviation or incorrect label will only confuse readers, in the same way that shoppers would be disorientated if they found the shampoo under the label *Dairy Products*.

Sometimes, because of constraints of stylistic balance, it is not possible to be absolutely specific with a label. However, where such limitations are not present you should be specific. Consider the following subheadings where the problem is a faulty valve.

1 Introduction
2 Purpose
3 Problem
4 Solutions
5 Recommendation

Since all the subheadings are of a general nature, it would be a stylistic imbalance to label section three 'Faulty Valve V260'.

Now consider the following subheadings of the development section of a report arguing that a new weekly shift system should not be introduced.

1 Purpose and Scope
2 Organization of the System
3 Financial Implications
4 Effect on Productivity Ratios
5 Employee Reaction to the System
6 Conclusions and Recommendations

As the financial implications were the only positive factors in this writer's discourse, it was appropriate to give section 3 the specific title, *Financial Implications*, rather than the more general label, *Advantages*. Since most professionals who must process pages of documents give a report or letter that initial scan, we might as well make it worth their while by using meaningful subheadings where and when we can.

Case study

Kate Rocard is in charge of the policies and procedures division of the hotels and leisure group, International Comfort Corporation S.A. She has been working on a new procedural policy and the following text forms the initial section of her report.

Select the most appropriate labels that Kate could use as subheadings from the options listed.

TITLE: AUTHORITY FOR ENGAGEMENT/AMENDMENT FORM

1.0 ___A___

    1.1 To define a procedure for processing the documentation required for recording on the Interpers and Payroll Systems the information on new staff joining International Comfort Corporation S.A.

    1.2 To ensure that the terms and conditions of employment are in accordance with the Corporation policies and procedures.

2.0 ___B___

    2.1 This procedure covers both Direct Hire and Seconded staff and includes all levels of staff of ICC.

    2.2 The Welfare Social Facilities staff who are under ICC administration are included in this procedure.

    2.3 Contractor personnel, either filling established posts or additional to establishment, are not put on these systems, and hence are excluded from this procedure.

3.0 ___C___

    3.1 The responsibility for finalizing the recruitment and selection process, preparing the Authority for Engagement/Amendment Form and approving the Authority for Engagement lies with the Recruitment and Selection Division.

    3.2 The Personnel Division is responsible for confirming that the terms and conditions of employment are in accordance with ICC policies. Preparing the contract documents and approving the Amendment Form is also a responsibility of the Personnel Division.

4.0 __*D*__

    4.1 The start of this procedure and the end of the recruitment selection process is indicated by the receipt within the Recruitment and Selection Division of either:

        4.1.1 Letter of Acceptance in the case of Direct Hire personnel or

        4.1.2 Staff Clearance Form from Hiltonia S.A. in the case of Seconded staff from Hiltonia S.A.

    4.2 On receipt of the above notification, an employee file with standard dividers is opened, and all correspondence to date related to the selected candidate is filed in the appropriate sections.

A schematic diagram showing the general flow of documentation is given in Appendix 1.

A	1	Problem
	2	Objectives
	3	Procedures
	4	Reasons for Procedures
	5	Modifications
B	1	Objectives
	2	Terms of Reference
	3	Purpose
	4	Scope
	5	Staff Involved
C	1	Procedure
	2	Selection Process
	3	Problem
	4	Finalization
	5	Responsibilities
D	1	Procedure
	2	Selection Process

3   Findings
4   Authority of Personnel
5   Modification of Forms

Answers   A2, B4, C5, D1

Paragraphs

In commercial texts there is a tendency to give paragraph status to each building block in an argument. This allows the reader to appreciate the information flow in a document. The usual approach to paragraph structure is to limit this language unit to one topic:

1st   **Introduce** the topic in the first sentence.

2nd   **Develop** the topic in clear and logically linked sentences.

3rd   **Conclude** the topic in the final sentence: this invariably contains the writer's main point.

If we look again at each subsection in the development of the report on clearing oil spills, you will note how the writer has applied this structure to the paragraphs. The first sentence introduces the topic while the final sentence expresses the main idea.

3.1 <u>Burning</u>

Attempts have been made to burn oil. Although wicking materials have been used to sustain burning on the sea, they have not been completely successful. It is not possible to burn oil on the beach without special equipment. Burning may be useful as a tool for dealing with fresh oil that comes ashore or in sheltered waters close to the shore. It is not an effective method for disposing of spilt oil.

3.2 <u>Sinking</u>

Sinking agents are used to sink oil by distributing a fine powder over the oil to increase its density. This is a difficult operation and it has been found that the sunken

oil reaches the sea bed in a form that might
well contaminate fishing gear and be detrimental
to bottom flora and fauna. Nevertheless, the
method can be improved by treating sand with
amine to make it oleophilic, and applying it as
a sand/water slurry. Both methods are effective,
but have disadvantages, and therefore should
only be used in emergency.

3.3 Booms

Booms may be used to prevent the spread of oil
over a wide area in the open sea or in calm
water. There are three methods of using the
booms: first, towed by a suitable tug, second,
moored in shallow water and, third, free
floating. The problem with all of these is that
oil escapes from underneath the boom. Moreover,
they cannot be used in rough conditions.
Although booms have proved useful in containing
oil for recovery, they are not 100% effective.

3.4 Dispersants

Dispersants are chemicals used for breaking up
spilt oil at sea and these have been found to be
the most satisfactory method of attack.
Achieving the best results with dispersant
chemicals depends upon two factors: first, the
distribution of an appropriate amount of the
chemical over the floating oil and, secondly,
the mixing or agitation of the treated oil with
the upper layer of the sea. Equipment which has
proved highly successful in performing the
mixing requirement is available and can be
fitted to any tug. Despite the huge quantity
used to break up floating oil on the open sea,
it causes negligible harm to marine life.

Review exercises

Exercise one

Study the following report, then complete the exercise that follows.

To: Technical Service Superintendent

From: Processing Engineering Section Head

Date: 29 April 19—

Subject: Evaluation of Amine Plate Heat
         Exchanger Chemical Cleaning

The plate heat exchanger (E–102) of unit 2 was
cleaned by using an in-house developed chemical
cleaning procedure. This operation was conducted
from 2 April to 5 April 19__ to enhance its
performance which in turn will improve energy
utilization efficiency.

1.0 Recommendations

    1.1 Conduct this chemical cleaning for all heat
        exchangers in the plant (Operation Section)

    1.2 Study the optimum frequency for chemical
        cleaning operation (Process Engineering)

    1.3 Approach the professional chemical cleaning
        companies to seek their advice on the
        following:

        – chemicals to be used
        – procedures to be adopted
        – chemical cleaning equipment to be
          incorporated.

2.0 Conclusions

    2.1 The chemical cleaning operation was
        conducted satisfactorily. However, there is
        still scope for improvement.

2.2 The efficiency of heat recovery improved from 65% before the cleaning to 85% after the cleaning.

2.3 The in-house chemical cleaning system is reliable.

3.0 Discussion

3.1 Amine Plate Exchanger Function

The amine plate exchanger (E-102) is one of those critical pieces of equipment for the gas treating unit. Its function is to recover the heat energy from the lean amine solution and to utilize it for the heating of the rich amine solution. This practice saves the company $5 million a year.

3.2 Pre-chemical Cleaning Status

3.2.1 It has been noticed that the performance of the heat exchanger decreased to about 65% of its design rate.

3.2.2 The temperature change across the lean amine side decreased from 50°C (design) to 32.5°C (currently experienced).

3.2.3 The pressure drop across the rich amine side has been increased from 0.1 bar (old experienced) to 0.2 bar (currently logged). The design pressure drop is 0.15 bar.

3.3 Post-chemical Cleaning Status

After conducting the chemical cleaning operation the following operating parameters were found:

3.3.1 The temperature change across the lean side was increased to 42.5°C.

3.3.2 The pressure drop across the rich amine side was reduced to 0.12 bar.

		Agree	*Disagree*
1	The subject heading is an appropriate label for this document.	[A]	[D]
2	The main subsections use general labels for subheadings.	[A]	[D]
3	The sub-subsections use specific labels.	[A]	[D]
4	The numbering system is consistent.	[A]	[D]
5	There is plenty of space surrounding each subsection.	[A]	[D]
6	The report is easy to scan because of the presentation techniques used by the writer.	[A]	[D]

You should tick A for each.

Exercise two

Study this memorandum, then assess the statements that follow.

To: All Branch Managers

From: Managing Director (Banking Services)

Subject: <u>Avona Feeds Ltd</u>

All managerial staff will be aware of the loss to
the bank caused by the bankruptcy of the above
company which was forced upon us by the current and
loan accounts recovering insufficient funds to
service the quarterly interest and commissions
charged, and to bring about a reduction in the
overall indebtedness to the bank. Had the manager
concerned followed the correct procedures detailed
in the Book of Instructions, and visited the client
on a regular basis, the fact that the company
accounts constantly showed a stock figure of
£100,000 would have been revealed to be fictitious
and the correct figure of approximately £1000 would
have been obvious. Reference to the maximum/minimum
computer report would also have indicated a cash

---

flow problem which, if acted upon, could have
reduced the bank's loss considerably. All Branch
Managers should ensure that their corporate
customers are visited regularly in accordance with
the guidelines in the Book of Instructions.

		Agree	Disagree
1	The document should have a date and reference.	[A]	[D]
2	The aim of the document is to notify all branch managers about the Avona Feeds Ltd account.	[A]	[D]
3	The information content relates to branch managers and their visits to corporate customers.	[A]	[D]
4	The managing director wishes to remind his readers of the importance of visits to corporate customers.	[A]	[D]
5	The aim as specified in the previous statement should be reflected in the subject heading.	[A]	[D]
6	'Guidelines in the Book of Instructions' would be an appropriate subject heading.	[A]	[D]
7	'Importance of Regular Visits to Corporate Customers' would be an appropriate subject heading.	[A]	[D]
8	The information is badly sequenced.	[A]	[D]
9	The tone of this text is far too direct for downward communication.	[A]	[D]
10	The style of the managing director's writing should be more informal.	[A]	[D]
11	From the beginning of the text itself, *All managerial staff will ...*, the managing director has used appropriate information control and language control.	[A]	[D]

	Agree	*Disagree*
12 The document requires a review focusing on	[A]	[D]
presentation techniques.		

Answers 1A 2D 3A 4A 5A 6D 7A 8D 9D 10D 11A 12A

Summary

The visual impact is usually the first aspect of your document to receive evaluation. It is therefore crucial for your purpose to ensure that you clear this hurdle without distracting your reader. At this point any serious judgement would invariably be negative. Your reader needs to access the information with ease, focus on your message quickly, and assimilate your ideas without undue effort. Given that you have accurately controlled the information and language aspects of your text, these reader-needs can be carefully satisfied by thoughtful use of techniques relating to visual (space, indentations and numbering system) and linguistic (labelling and paragraph structure) presentation.

9 Describing a sequence of actions

Since written documentation is an expression of a continuous flow of related thoughts, it is important that your readers are assisted through the text of your discourse without having to work out these relationships for themselves. In conversation, if this relationship is not fully comprehended, listeners can seek clarification or test assumed associations. Readers do not have the advantage of explanations concerning the interaction of ideas in your text, nor indeed should they require them. The words we use to link ideas are referred to as *connectives*. They have two major and essential functions: first, they bring flow and cohesion to your thought patterns and, second, they are signposts which help in the assimilation process by indicating concession, addition, contrast, cause and effect relationships, etc. Without these indicators your readers would be lost.

Connectives

Consider the following text:

> A slowdown occurred in the bank's business momentum
> during the second half of 1989. The last fiscal year
> was an excellent one for the German banks as a
> whole. Results were expected by analysts as well as
> investors. Bank shares experienced a sharp decline
> for the first ten months of the year. The market
> lost 20.4% between 1 January and 19 March. Bank
> shares came even further down.
>
> Banks are an integrated part of the economy. Their
> performance reflects the state of total business
> activities of a country. A downturn in general
> economic expectations will have a strong negative
> impact on estimated bank earnings. German banks are
> operating in a universal banking environment. They

> are viewed by the investing community as a
> homogeneous group. Bank stocks should move in the
> same direction at almost the same percentage figure.

It seems that each sentence is an isolated idea having little or no meaning in any cohesive context. However, once we insert connectives to show the relationships, the text is cohesive, logical and easily understood.

> Despite a slowdown in the bank's business momentum
> during the second half of 1989, the last fiscal year
> was an excellent one for the German banks as a
> whole. Although these results were expected by
> analysts as well as investors, bank shares
> experienced a sharp decline for the first ten months
> of the year. When the market lost 20.4% between 1
> January and 19 March, bank shares came even further
> down.
>
> Banks are an integrated part of the economy and
> therefore their performance reflects the state of
> total business activities of a country.
> Consequently, a downturn in general economic
> expectations will have a strong negative impact on
> estimated bank earnings. Furthermore, German banks
> are operating in a universal banking environment,
> therefore they are viewed by the investing community
> as a homogeneous group. Consequently, bank stocks
> should move in the same direction at almost the same
> percentage figure.

Here the relationships between the sentences have been made explicit. In this particular text, the writer is supporting a main idea: the parallels in banking performance and national economic performance. He is elaborating an argument, so he must appeal to the reader's sense of logic. To do this he has used words like:

although
despite
consequently

furthermore
moreover
therefore
at the same time

These connecting words are essential if you wish to achieve a logical flow of ideas. The type of connective device you will need will depend on the nature and function of the document you have to produce.

In an argumentative text you will need to:

- add
- contrast
- concede
- show cause and effect relationships
- refer to ideas previously expressed.

In a narrative or progress report you will also need to:

- sequence ideas
- show time relationships
- change from topic to topic.

In procedural reports or instrumental documents you will certainly need to employ sequence markers.

If you categorize all the functions of linking words, the most frequently used vocabulary falls into eight main groups.

1   Addition

furthermore, as well as, not only ... but also, moreover, in addition (to), also, besides, and

This group is used for adding items of information together. The connectives listed here have a similar function to the mathematical symbol $+$.

e.g. Prextel has a very high compound rate of growth *and* its solidity is a reflection of a highly conservative accounting policy.

2   Concession/contrast

however, although, in contrast, yet, nevertheless, but, none the less, despite this, in spite of, even though, still

Where two ideas contrast, this can be made clear for the reader by using a connective like *but*.

e.g. Finance companies are discreet in extending credit, *but* the borrower has never before had a better opportunity.

Where the second idea is rather surprising or unexpected in relation to the first, a useful connective is *nevertheless*.

e.g. Rokia appears to be satisfied with its present product line. *Nevertheless*, it has made attempts to widen its range to include more specialized products.

3   Alternatives

on the other hand, alternatively, again, another possibility, (n)either ... (n)or
    These connectives are used when the writer wants to make it clear that alternatives are being described.
e.g. Investment opportunities can be considered in the local area *or* on a global scale.

4   Cause/effect

because (of), owing to, due to, hence, as a consequence, as a result, consequently, therefore, so
    These connectives are used to show cause/effect relationships.
    When the effect is followed by the cause:

The rise in interest rates was delayed	*because of* *owing to* *due to*	a sudden fall in the value of the dollar.

    When the cause is followed by the effect:

There was a sudden fall in the value of the dollar.	*Therefore,* *As a consequence,* *Hence,* *Consequently,* *For this reason,* *As a result,*	a rise in interest rates was delayed.

5   Introduction of a new topic

As regards, regarding, with regard to, with reference to, with respect to, in terms of, as for, as to, by the way, incidentally, now
    There are many expressions used for introducing a new topic. The use of these expressions gives a flow to the text and reminds the reader that you are now considering a different issue.
e.g. Most of the causes for the loss in trade are now clear. *As regards* the action to be taken, no decisions have yet been made.
    There are few differences between the two computers. The ICN model is slightly smaller, but *with respect to* cost, the two are comparable.

6   Labelling

for example, as a suggestion, in brief, finally, to conclude, to sum up, in conclusion

In your reading you will notice that some expressions are used to move from one idea to another. The expression introduces and labels the subsequent idea. This is very common in business texts.

for example: followed by an example
as a suggestion: followed by a suggestion
in brief: followed by a summary

e.g. Many options are open. *For example*, we could sell some shares.

To sum up, a system could be arranged for implementation on site.

7   Back reference

this/these, it/they, the latter, the former

When it is important for the writer to show the reader relationships between sentences/ideas, there are several techniques used where one idea provides a link by referring back to a previous idea or word.

e.g.

1   The pound is strengthening. *It* is also expected to continue on this upward trend.
2   Banks had a dull day. *They* all reported minimal losses.
3   Between the post office and the National Bank is a large tower. *This* edifice is the official stock market building.
4   The new building was opened by the city mayor. *This* will house the official documents.
5   Lock the computer and secure the key. *This* will ensure no information is retrieved illicitly.
6   The heat will cause the water to evaporate. *This* process . . .

8   Sequence markers

firstly/secondly, then/next, subsequently/after, prior to/before, at the same time/while

The obvious sequence markers are numbers and these are necessary for many documents that give instructions or procedures. Consider the following document.

```
To:       Brian Carroll, Production Manager
From:     John Haig, Senior Maintenance Engineer
Date:     January 8, 19__
Subject: Proposed Work During 'A' Train Shutdown

During the upcoming 'A' train shutdown, it may be
necessary to shut in the Faroah 'B' platform. In
order to maintain gas manifold pressure, the
following work should be completed.

1. Standardize swing rope brackets.
2. Seal weld production separator flowline braces to
   decking.
3. Seal weld around perimeter of hatchway.
4. Seal weld air receiver tank to decking.
5. Cut off gaitronics mounting plate.
6. Modify sump tank overboard vent line.
7. Install multi-voltage outlet mounting plate.
```

This is not an exclusive list of connectives. Furthermore, the options under each grouping are interchangeable. Selection will most certainly be determined by the grammatical context. As a writer you will need access to all these connective devices.

Exercise

How would you complete the following passages? Use these nine words and phrases to fill the gaps in the text:

and	despite
however	but
although	on the other hand
both	also
and	

Comparing Computers

_____ the IBM _____ the Amstrad will run the same software. The IBM is very well made _____ the Amstrad is much cheaper. _____ being so cheap the Amstrad is _____ much faster than the

IBM _____ has more memory. _____ the IBM has better after-sales service _____ this is expensive. _____ the Amstrad has a very good record of reliability.

Now compare your selections with those offered here:

Both the IBM and the Amstrad will run the same software. The IBM is very well made but the Amstrad is much cheaper. Despite being so cheap the Amstrad is also much faster than the IBM and has more memory. On the other hand, the IBM has better after-sales service although this is expensive. However, the Amstrad has a very good record of reliability.

In a similar way, use these words and phrases to fill the gaps in the text below:

the latter	because
as regards	for example
therefore	this
in terms of	either
or	

_____ after-sales service the IBM is much better than the Amstrad. _____ IBM guarantee a replacement within 24 hours but Amstrad only give a parts guarantee. _____ we need all our machines to be working every day _____ is very important. _____ we should buy _____ four IBM machines _____ five Amstrad machines so that we have a spare available. _____ price _____ is the best choice.

Now compare your selections with those offered here.

As regards after-sales service the IBM is much better than the Amstrad. For example, IBM guarantee a replacement within 24 hours but Amstrad only give a parts guarantee. Because we need all our machines to be working every day, this is very important. Therefore, we should buy either four IBM machines or five Amstrad machines so that we have a spare available. In terms of price, the latter is the best choice.

Case study

Bernard Laurent is an associate director of Savaction/Paris, international consultants in industrial psychology.

Melloux Corporation produces engine parts for Airospace Inc. Recently the president of Airospace, Jon Knight, has complained on several occasions to the managing director of Melloux, Paul Barnes, about the increased incidence of poor-quality parts, missed deadlines and lack of sensitivity to Airospace requirements.

Paul Barnes requested Savaction to investigate and monitor the working practices at Melloux and report back to him ... on paper.

Bernard has concluded the investigation and the monitoring which formed the basis of his operational task. He has also completed the first two phases of the reporting task: thinking and planning. This is the outcome—his topic outline.

1.0 <u>Introduction</u>

   Who?   Savaction, Paris
   What?   Requested to monitor work
             behaviour/examine operational environment
   Where? At the Melloux Corporation
   When? October 15 to October 29, 19__
   Why?   To ascertain causes of deterioration in
             working practices.

2.0 <u>Working Conditions</u>

   – Operations area – cramped floor layout.
   – Gloves and boots – clumsy so hardly ever worn.
   – Ventilation in operations area rather poor.
   – Equipment is out of date.

3.0 <u>Considerations of Safety</u>

   – Safety checks are irregular.
   – Code is not properly implemented.
   – There are no safety posters displayed.
   – Supervisors are too busy to check safety
     practice.

4.0 <u>Manpower Problems</u>

   – Morale is low among the workforce.
   – Training of unskilled labour is non-existent.
   – Turnover of labour – 35% over last 12 months.

5.0 <u>Supervisory Problems</u>

   – Supervisors are not given management support.
   – Supervisors are definitely overworked.
   – They are low in motivation.

– The workforce has more than doubled in the
last year.
– The number of supervisors is the same as last
year.
– Little respect from workforce towards
supervisors.

6.0 <u>Conclusions</u>

– Workforce lacks motivation.
– Safety standards – low.
– Attitudes are non-productive.
– There is no cohesive force.
– Productivity will continue to fall.

7.0 <u>Recommendations</u>

– Set up a training programme covering:
technical operations
safety procedures
– Review policies on:
working conditions
performance appraisals
– Define ratios of supervisors to workforce.
– Implement a safety campaign so that the
workforce becomes more safety conscious.

With the outline already worked out, Bernard's writing task, as far
as information control is concerned (i.e. the content and sequence), is
now complete.

Bernard now needs to decide on the tone he will adopt, be sensitive
to the eight points of formal written style, and ensure the written
expression of his ideas is not hampered by superfluous verbiage.

There is one other issue that Bernard must tackle, a language
issue—namely, ensuring that all his sentences are properly linked. If he
does this task correctly, the reader will be helped through the document
in the same way that a car driver, new to a foreign city, is helped by
signposts to reach her destination.

This is Bernard's report. Can you identify the connectives he has
used?

To: Paul Barnes   Date: 21 January 19__
           Managing Director
           Melloux Corporation

From: Bernard Laurent   Ref: MC/326
           Associate Director
           Savaction

Subject: Evaluation of Working Practices at Melloux
           Corporation

In order to ascertain causes of deterioration in
working practices at Melloux Corporation, Savaction
was requested to monitor work behaviour and examine
the operational environment. This was conducted from
15 to 29 October 19__.

With regard to the working conditions, it was
observed that the operations area is not only
cramped but also rather badly ventilated.
Furthermore, the workers seem to be working with
out-of-date equipment. For example, the prescribed
gloves and boots are seldom worn because they are
clumsy and cumbersome.

As for considerations of safety, checks are
irregular, the code is not properly implemented and,
finally, posters are not displayed. In addition, it
was noticed that supervisors lack the time to check
safety practices.

Manpower problems are highlighted by the low morale
of the workforce. This is helped by the fact that
not only is the turnover of labour high — 35% over
the last year — but also that training of unskilled
labour is non-existent.

Regarding the problems experienced by the
supervisors, it is obvious that in addition to being
overworked, they receive little support from
management. As a consequence they are not motivated
and receive little respect from the workforce.
Finally, despite the fact that the workforce has

doubled in the last year, the number of supervisors has remained the same.

To conclude, the following are the major reasons for the deterioration in working practices at Melloux:

- the entire workforce lacks motivation
- safety standards are low
- attitudes are non-productive
- there is no cohesive force.

For these reasons it is obvious that, under present conditions, productivity will continue to suffer.

It is strongly recommended that a training programme be set up to cover both technical operations and safety procedures. Furthermore, there should be an immediate review of policies relating to working conditions, performance appraisals and definitions of ratios relating supervisors to workforce. In conclusion, a safety campaign ought to be implemented so that the workforce becomes more safety conscious.

Because Bernard Laurent has used effective connecting words, use of labels as subheadings would be superfluous. Note the tautology in the following examples:

Considerations of safety
As for considerations of safety, checks ...

Supervisory problems
Regarding the problems experienced by the supervisors, it is ...

Recommendations
It is strongly recommended that ...

One of the recommendations in this report was to review the performance appraisal programme of Melloux Corporation. Paul Barnes, the managing director, was so surprised at the content of this report that he immediately authorized Gerry Sexton, his personnel manager, to organize a performance appraisal programme in collaboration with Savaction.

Gerry had to keep his managing director informed of the progress he was making in this direction. Below is a section of a progress report dated 4 February 19__. The connectives have been deleted. Indicate which option you would choose by circling your choice.

Note: Because this is a progress report the majority of the connectives will be sequence markers.

---

(1)____ the week November 20–25, 19__ a representative of Savaction, Mr Bernard Laurent, accompanied by two members of the Personnel Department, held discussions and interviews with department representatives of all levels, including managers, superintendents and selected supervisors. (2)____ focused primarily on current performance appraisal practices and problem areas. (3)____ also covered a general review of alternative approaches to the existing system.

(4)____ that week, a meeting chaired by Mr Laurent had been held at the Savaction offices with senior members of the Personnel Department. (5)____ focused on the existing performance appraisal system and procedures. The meeting also included a review of the company's training policy.

On November 25, 19__, Mr Laurent held a meeting with all members of the management. (6)____ a briefing on the main findings of previous discussions with various departments, general management directives were obtained on certain basic aspects of the intended Performance Appraisal Programme. At this meeting the visiting consultant emphasized the need for training in:
– conducting performance interviews, and
– discussing job description contents with the
  employees concerned.

(7)____ the submission of the first version of the Performance Appraisal Programme by Savaction, which included three sections, namely:
– Performance Appraisal
– Potential Appraisal
– Merit Appraisal

several meetings were held by senior staff from the Personnel Department during which the programme was discussed in detail. A summary of this meeting was then sent to Savaction for consideration.

(8) _____ all department managers were advised of:
- Savaction's programme
- the Personnel Department's views
- the new on-the-job training programme.

(9) _____ each manager contributed to a constructive discussion in the realization that this programme had been developed to achieve optimum productivity within each department.

Following the receipt of the department manager's feedback, two meetings were held with the Personnel Department and the results of the detailed discussions were sent to Savaction for consideration.

(10) _____ all these efforts, Savaction has recently submitted a second version of the Performance Appraisal Programme. (11) _____ has incorporated all the remarks, comments and points of view raised by the company's departments that were deemed appropriate. Savaction has (12) _____ accepted an invitation to review our new on-the-job training programme which is now a part of the whole package.

1	a.	during	b.	before	c.	regarding
2	a.	these	b.	this	c.	they
3	a.	these	b.	this	c.	they
4	a.	although	b.	prior to	c.	after
5	a.	it	b.	this	c.	besides
6	a.	during	b.	at the same time	c.	after
7	a.	after	b.	then	c.	furthermore
8	a.	then	b.	at the same time	c.	because
9	a.	although	b.	however	c.	furthermore
10	a.	in addition	b.	as a result of	c.	therefore
11	a.	this	b.	it	c.	they
12	a.	however	b.	also	c.	again

1A, 2A, 3C, 4B, 5B, 6C, 7A, 8B, 9C, 10B, 11A, 12B

Exercises

The following is an extract from the beginning of an investment appraisal. It is therefore an argumentative text. Provide suitable connectives, where necessary, then compare your version with the suggestions given in the key.

SUMMARY

Pelsevier holds a special place among Danish quoted companies. (1)____ it has the highest profit margins. (2)____ it is the only one that has consistently increased both its operating profit margin and its return on capital employed over the last five years. (3)____ EPS has grown at least 20% a year — for the last twenty years.

Management has not only maximized the highest yielding operations within the group (4)____has also cut back on those which have not met its exacting requirements with a ruthless efficiency not seen in most other Danish companies. (5)____ it now has considerable reserves and an exceptionally solid balance sheet.

(6)____ the future, Pelsevier operates in fairly mature and competitive markets. (7)____ this, it still has the scope for further profit growth. (8)____ acquisitions have been and will be vital for growth, they are becoming more expensive. (9)____ this, management is constantly searching for ideas and new investments. One of these was the Loukar investment.

(10)____ for the next two years, Pelsevier's 20% annual increase in EPS is likely to be maintained.

In summary, it can be said for Pelsevier that over the next two years:

- its annual increase in EPS is likely to be maintained.
- its hitherto brilliant management will have continued success against increasing challenges.

– it will continue to achieve better growth than
  most other major Danish companies.

RECOMMENDATION

Pelsevier's shares are – like the general market –
very weak at present. (11)____ they are still among
the most highly rated, reflecting the market's
expectations for above-average EPS growth. Another
reason for their weakness is that Pelsevier has
received adverse publicity in the national press
following its attempt to buy Loukar. It is felt that
Loukar is a good investment which will contribute
positively to EPS from this year, and that the
criticism has been overstated. (12)____ the shares
should rise in line with the recovery market.
(13)____ they are a strong BUY.

Key

Your choice may not be the same as the key. However, each of your
selections should belong to the same group of connectives as the answers
given below (see the eight groups discussed earlier in this chapter).

1 For example	7 Despite
2 Furthermore	8 Although
3 Moreover	9 Because of
4 But	10 Accordingly
5 As a result	11 Despite this
6 As for	12 Therefore
	13 Consequently

Instructions

In the exercise above you will have used linking devices for arguing/
persuading, e.g. *moreover, therefore, furthermore, although*. When you
need to describe a sequence of actions, as in instructions, procedures or
processes, it is better not to use sequence markers – *then, after this,
before, prior to, next* – but rather to keep to numbers. In the following
text, note that the writer always begins the instruction with the verb.
This is a similar style to that used in the instructional text on page 146.
Here the text is a list of instructions in the form of a recipe.

How to prepare slices of fish coated with a sweet
and spicy masala paste and fried in a generous
amount of oil.
  Once you have the ingredients:
   1. Mix salt into masala paste.
   2. Wash slices of fish.
   3. Coat slices evenly with paste.
   4. Allow fish to stand for 2 to 3 hours.
   5. Heat oil or ghee in a frying pan.
   6. Place slices of fish in pan.
   7. Turn over fish when cooked.
   8. Cook other side.
   9. Spoon the hot oil over fish in serving dish.
  10. Serve immediately.

If you are in a position of responsibility then it is inevitable that you will be called upon at some time to confirm delegated work by issuing written instructions. The efficient running of any organization/department depends, to a great extent, upon effective communication, especially when instructions have to be given. It is therefore important to ensure the recipient is fully aware of exactly *what* you want done, *where*, *when* and *why*. To ensure the sequence of actions is clearly understood it is advisable to begin each instruction with the verb. The form of the verb in an instruction is the *imperative mood* as demonstrated in the recipe for preparing the fish dish. Occasionally, a description of the consequences of an action, or a piece of advice, or a warning, or even a regulation will be necessary. When this is required, the appropriate modal verb should be used.

Consider the following unrelated instructions. Note that each instruction begins with the imperative form of the verb. Indicate the function of the modal verbs, printed in italics.

1. Pour the boiling water onto the tea. The teapot *should* be preheated.
   (order, warning, consequence, advice)
2. Paint the refurbished woodwork. A bright colour *must* be used.
   (order, warning, consequence, advice)
3. Remove the safety valve. This valve *must* be left on site.
   (order, warning, consequence, advice)
4. Press 'Ctrl' and 'Enter' keys together. The VDU *will* display a list of options.
   (order, warning, consequence, advice)

5. Instruct the passenger on the advertised fare. When the flight is full discounts *must not* be given.
   (order, warning, consequence, advice)
6. Boil the mixture for half an hour. The dish *should* be stirred at least every five minutes.
   (order, warning, consequence, advice)
7. Write the passenger's name on the ticket. A ball-point pen *must* be used.
   (order, warning, consequence, advice)
8. Enter the credit card details. The expiry date *should not* be after the date of the return flight.
   (order, warning, consequence, advice)
9. Lock all doors and windows securely before leaving the office. Non-compliance *could* lead to dismissal.
   (order, warning, consequence, advice)
10. Switch on the electricity. The machine *will* be ready for use.
    (order, warning, consequence, advice)
11. Ensure visitors wear earmuffs. Eardrum damage *may* be caused by too much exposure to the high-pitched noise.
    (order, warning, consequence, advice)
12. Obey these instructions. Non-conformity with the sequence *could* result in permanent injury or damage.

Key

1 Advice	2 Order	3 Order
4 Consequence	5 Order	6 Advice
7 Order	8 Advice	9 Warning
10 Consequence	11 Warning	12 Warning

Exercise

When Gerry Sexton, personnel manager of Melloux Corporation, received the instructions from his managing director, Paul Barnes, to collaborate with Savaction, he issued the following plan of action. Could you improve this document?

```
First, discussions will be held with Savaction.
After these discussions we shall determine our
current performance appraisal procedures. Then we
shall document any significant feedback with these
```

procedures. On completion of this task we shall
coordinate our activities with those of Savaction.

We will then be in a position to prepare material
for a training course on principles and techniques
of performance appraisals. This course will
subsequently be implemented for all supervisors. By
June 19__ all workers should have been interviewed.

Now compare your version with the following:

1. Hold discussions with Savaction.
2. Determine current performance appraisal
   procedures.
3. Document significant feedback.
4. Coordinate activities with Savaction.
5. Prepare materials for performance appraisal
   training course.
6. Implement course for all supervisors.
7. Ensure all workers have been appraised by June
   19__.

It is important, when writing instructions, that the reader under-
stands clearly, comprehensively and accurately, exactly what is
required. In certain working situations—for example, when working
with dangerous machinery or when prescribing medicine to a patient—
one incorrect instruction could result in serious injury or even death.
   When writing instructions:

1. Number for purposes of clarity.
2. Use the imperative mood to ensure the exact activity to be performed
   is clearly understood.
3. Explain the consequences of each action where and when necessary.
4. Give advice, warning or regulation using the passive form of the
   appropriate modal verb.

Summary

Ideas are expressed in a sequence of words. In speech, a series of words
can be seen to form a cohesive image, picture or argument through body
language, intonation patterns and vocal pitch. In writing, we must use

language techniques referred to as connectives. These devices help the writer by giving cohesion and flow to the ideas expressed on paper. They help the reader by being used as signposts indicating relationships of concession, addition, contrast, cause and effect and alternatives. Finally, connectives assist the assimilation of a sequence or a change of topic.

10 Writing letters and recording discussions

The 'S' of the SOLDIER anagram relates to whether the author projects a sensitive image. A writer needs to respect the feelings, beliefs and cultural alignment of the reader. The production of two particular business documents requires a very careful approach.

Documents which project not only your own personal image but also that of your company are different from internal memoranda and reports. Business letters are clearly examples of person-to-person communication that project a company image.

The other example of a document requiring care in production because of the sensitivity issue is the reporting of conversations. Misquotes and/or misinterpretations can occasion conflict, criticism and consternation. It is therefore useful to be acquainted with the armoury required to project clearly the sensitive, decisive and responsible aspects of your image.

Letter writing

Success in business writing depends, without doubt, on your ability to be reader friendly as well as achieve your writing purpose. This is important when your writing task is not just a written transaction *within* your organization but one that takes on an ambassadorial function for the reader who is *outside* your organization. This is why letter writing ought to be treated separately. The principal difference between letter writing and other business writing tasks is that the reader and the writer become as important as the topic of the document. People, not methods, machines or modifications, must receive the focus of attention. Feelings and emotions need to be addressed. Organizations do not communicate with organizations: people communicate with people.

Consider the following memo, which was written by the managing director of an advertising company to one of his account managers, Jane Morris.

To: Jane Morris

From: Nigel Owen

Date: 20 July 19__

Subject: Payment of Bostack Invoice No. SP699

Payment of this invoice is well overdue. Contact should be made immediately with John Lewis, the Bostack Finance Manager, in an effort to secure payment before 31 July.

It is essential that a record is kept of all invoice dates. Reminders should be sent at regular intervals to ensure payment is received within ninety days of the invoice date.

Your prompt action in this regard would be appreciated.

One of Nigel's reasons for issuing this memo was to ensure payment of the invoice before 31 July. The tone is appropriate: it is downward, direct and demanding. Jane now has to write a letter which will have a similar aim: to persuade Mr Lewis to pay the invoice before the end of July. She wrote the letter that appears below. Note that the topic is the same as Nigel Owen's memo.

COMELY ADVERTISING

27 Brent Road, Bolton, Lancs, BS6 6SQ

21 July 19__

Bostack Ltd
163 Housing Row
Riponsdale
Yorkshire BD17 2GR

Dear Mr Lewis,

<u>Invoice No. SP699</u>

Our records show that we have not received payment of this invoice dated 29 March 19__.

I will be in Riponsdale next week. Perhaps I could
call on you to discuss any problems you have
regarding acknowledgement of our invoice.

Could you phone me before Friday to let me know if
10.0 o'clock on Monday 27th would be convenient?

I look forward to hearing from you.

Yours sincerely,

Jane Morris
Account Manager

A comparison of the memo and the letter reveals that the most significant difference is in style and tone. Jane's letter does have the same ultimate aim as Nigel's memo. The letter, however, is far more reader-oriented. The focus is on person to person, not the invoice, as was the case with the memo. The tone is friendly and warm. Personal pronouns abound in the letter whereas Nigel uses the style appropriate to his reader's situation: inter-office. Had Jane used a similar style and tone in her letter Mr Lewis would have been annoyed and Jane would not have secured a meeting for Monday. This fictitious case is based on a real-life issue where payment was made before Friday 24 July! The cheque was accompanied by the following letter:

BOSTACK LTD
163 Housing Row, Riponsdale, Yorkshire, BD17 2GR

22 July 19__

Dear Ms Morris,

Invoice No. SP699

Thank you for your letter dated 21 July 19__.

Please find enclosed a cheque for £18,642.72.

We are extremely sorry for the late payment of your
invoice. This was due to a modification in our
computerized processing procedure. I apologise for
any inconvenience.

You are quite welcome to call into our office next
Monday. Unfortunately, I shall be in London all next
week but Jaz Martin, our new advertising manager,
would like to discuss a project we are considering
for a Spring '9_ launch.

Once again I apologise for any inconvenience.

Yours sincerely,

John Lewis
Manager: Finance

Enc: Cheque No. 0076283

Here again we can note the style and tone of John Lewis's letter: friendly, warm and sincere. Focus is once more on person to person.

The presentation of letters is very important. First impressions are usually correct so you should use the layout of your letter as an ally. Try to refer to the reader early in the letter and, unless you wish to impose your authority, the *I* should not receive priority over the pronoun *you*.

Begin with a positive impact and end with goodwill. This policy should be used even in letters bearing a negative import, e.g. letters of regret, criticism or refusal. Indeed, for business letter writing in general, you should follow the ABC rule—**A**ccurate, **B**rief and **C**ourteous.

Would you consider any changes to the following letter?

Dear Sir,

Valves AS211 and AS231

It is regretted that the order required is currently
out of stock.

The next delivery of this line is expected by the
end of September.

This office should be contacted before 21 September
if the required items are still deemed necessary.

Yours faithfully,

R. S. Chambers

This letter may be accurate and brief but it certainly is not courteous. No reference is made to the reader nor to his request for the valves. Goodwill is missing at the end of the letter so the recipient could quite easily look elsewhere for the items. A more acceptable version would apply all the points raised so far in this chapter. Before you read the variation below, why not produce your own for comparative purposes?

```
Dear Sir,

Valves AS211 and AS231

Thank you for your order dated 21 August 19__.

Unfortunately, we are currently out of stock of
these particular valves.

We are expecting a delivery by the end of September.
Should you still require these valves perhaps you
could confirm by letting me know before 21 September.

Once again we are sorry for any inconvenience and
look forward to receiving your confirmation.

Yours faithfully,


R. S. Chambers
```

Exercise

Which phrases suit the style and tone of a letter? Tick either suitable or unsuitable.

		Suitable	Unsuitable
1	I would continue using this remedy during the next maintenance overhaul.	[ ]	[ ]
2	It is recommended that this remedy is used during the next maintenance overhaul.	[ ]	[ ]
3	Your letter relating to this matter has been received.	[ ]	[ ]

		Suitable	Unsuitable
4	Thank you for your letter on this matter.	[v]	[ ]
5	It is felt that any progress should be carefully monitored.	[ ]	[ ]
6	I think you should carefully monitor any progress.	[ ]	[ ]
7	I am pleased you are able to accept our invitation.	[ ]	[ ]
8	It is hereby acknowledged that the invitation has been accepted.	[ ]	[ ]
9	An early response would be appreciated.	[ ]	[ ]
10	I would appreciate your response as early as possible.	[ ]	[ ]
11	You could raise this issue at our next scheduled meeting so that we can resolve this problem together.	[ ]	[ ]
12	This issue ought to be raised during the next scheduled meeting when a solution could be reached which is acceptable to both parties.	[ ]	[ ]

Answers 1S   2U   3U   4S   5U   6S
        7S   8U   9U   10S   11S   12U

You will notice, if your selections agree with those suggested, that the impersonal style and the hard tone are not normally used for business letters. Accent is on reader friendliness when our written communication is *between companies*.

Recording business discussions

An observation often made at meetings is that, when the convener asks someone to take the minutes, all present simultaneously have something wrong with their shoes! Eye contact, in other words, would undoubtedly be interpreted as a willingness to record the proceedings. Most people are happier when the secretary takes the minutes, as would normally , happen at formal business meetings.

Many of our business meetings are *ad hoc* affairs, yet the decisions

are weighty enough to warrant the production of a document. Marketing personnel, company representatives and contractors often find that
their operational tasks have suddenly evolved, quite unintentionally,
into a negotiating session where the outcome, and the process by which
the outcome was reached, call for the production of a document usually
referred to as the minutes of a meeting.

In a similar way, the banker's call memo, the doctor's patient record
and the supervisor's counselling report are all examples of a written
record of a conversation.

The majority of people find this duty particularly difficult because it
requires, in many cases, an ability to participate meaningfully in a
discussion while at the same time activating the mental skills and
resources to record *who* said *what*, *when* and *why*. A few techniques both
in the taking of notes of a conversation and the production of the record
can make these exercises less onerous and distressing.

With note taking, the important issue is to decide what information
is essential for recording purposes. A large part of our conversational
transactions contains superfluous information merely to sustain the
logic of an argument.

The logical outcome of a discussion—the conclusion, decision, professional recommendation, etc.—is invariably the important issue for
the record books.

Exercise

Consider the following report. It was written to inform the reader about
a very serious meeting which was held in the office of the head of
maintenance of an oil-producing company at an offshore location.

An accident had occurred when a visiting supply barge hit a main support
leg of the south pier, which connects the accommodation platform to the
operations platform. The precise location for repair work was designated as
a hazardous area. Specialist work was required. The contractor's representative was present at the meeting, which lasted two hours. Jim Stack, the
operations superintendent, produced the following memo for his boss, Reg
Peacock, manager of operations.

To: Reg Peacock   Ref: 86/P/90
         Manager of Operations
From: Jim Stack   Date: April 6, 19__
         Operations Superintendent

Subject: <u>Repair Arrangements to the South Pier</u>

A meeting was held at 0930 hours on 5 April 19__ to
discuss arrangements for the repair work on the
South Pier. The meeting was held in the office of
the Head of Maintenance. The following personnel
were present:

Bill Stanley, Head of Maintenance
David Barnevik, Head of Fire and Safety
Willi Mischak, Envian Incorp. (contractor
representative)
Jacques Simon, Platform Operations Superintendent
John Sculley, Marine Services Engineer
Jim Stack, Operations Superintendent

1. It is estimated that the work will require 21
   days to complete. (Shift rotation 24 hours a
   day).

2. The contractor will begin work on Saturday, 11
   April 19__.

3. A barge will be used to accommodate contractor's
   personnel during the repair work period.

4. A company maintenance foreman and safety officer
   will be available on site at all times.

5. Smoking will only be permitted on the barge.

6. Any practices or situations observed by company
   or contractor personnel and thought to be
   potentially dangerous will be reported to the
   Company Safety Officer immediately.

7. Envian Incorporated will produce a daily progress
   report each morning and notify the Head of
   Maintenance of any radical changes to the planned
   schedule.

The meeting ended at mid-day.

Here Jim has relayed only the essential information. Notice that each sentence is structured in the form of a decision for the future, e.g. 'A barge *will be used*'. This is customary for the writer of business discussions when decisions or policies are being made.

A more formal minutes of a meeting would normally be written to a company-designed format. Compare Jim Stack's report with the record of a meeting held in the same oil company but this time on the mainland.

The oil is pumped to a tank farm. The municipality had decided in 19__ to build a major highway between the oil terminal and the tank farm. Obviously, it was planned that the road would traverse the main pipeline network so regular progress meetings had to be held between the oil company, the contractors and the municipality. Here are the minutes of one of the liaison meetings.

COBIL OIL COMPANY

RECORD OF MEETING NO: 36

TOPIC: Highway　　　DATE OF MEETING: 26 July 19__
Development in Scot bay

LOCATION: Cobil H.Q. TIME: from 10:00 to 13:30

PURPOSE: Progress　　CONVENOR: Barbara Chambers,
　　　　　　　　　　　　　　　　Cobil Liaison Officer

PRESENT:　　　　　　　DESIGNATION/COMPANY

1. Barbara Chambers Liaison Officer, Cobil
2. Peter Jordan　　　Admin. Officer, Cobil
3. Percy Hallock　　 Construction Engineer, Meredith
　　　　　　　　　　　Ltd.
4. Fred Taylor　　　 Design Consultant, Eulan Incorp.
5. John Fields　　　 Municipality Officer, Local
　　　　　　　　　　　Council

ITEM	DISCUSSION	ACTION BY
1	**Temporary Bridge in Zone F** Cobil advised Eulan to contact Field Maintenance for design specifications regarding fill under the bridge.	Eulan

ITEM	DISCUSSION	ACTION BY
2	**Excavation Lines in Zone B** These lines had been traversed by Meredith's heavy machinery. Cobil insisted that Meredith excavate under Cobil supervision. Meredith promised to notify on dates and times.	Meredith
3	**Drainage Ditches in Zone C** Plans for the ditches were presented by Eulan. Cobil asked for plans showing how the pipelines would be affected. Eulan promised these by the following week.	Eulan
4	**Presentation and Dating of Drawings** The Municipality requested an early presentation of drawings to ensure a full analysis before granting approval.	Eulan
5	**New Culvert in Zone A** The design and drawings were to be made available for discussion at a later date. The meeting adjourned at 13:30.	Eulan

Here you will notice that Peter Jordan, the Cobil administrative officer who wrote the record of the discussion, has limited the information to the essential and discarded the arguments which must have preceded the decisions recorded. Peter has used three techniques which have produced this commonly found style of reporting discussions.

1 He has used reported speech structure, i.e. the verbs are in the past tense and time references are changed.

John Fields: 'I want to see the drawings'
becomes

'The Municipality *requested* ...'

Fred Taylor: 'I'll let you have the drawings so that we can discuss the design tomorrow'
becomes
'The design and drawings were *to be made* available for discussion on the *following day*'.

Fred Taylor: 'I'll let you have the drawings next week'
becomes
'Eulan *promised* these by the *following week*'.

2 He has used suitable introductory verbs.

'I'll give them to you next week.'
This is introduced by:
'He *promised* ...'

'If I were you, I'd contact Field Maintenance.'
This is introduced by:
'Cobil *advised* ...'

'You must excavate those lines manually.'
This is introduced by:
'Cobil *insisted* ...'

Here is a list of the common introductory verbs used in recording conversations:

said	told	accused
asked	requested	affirmed
suggested	ordered	persisted
promised	stated	confirmed
informed	imagined	admitted
predicted	recommended	demanded
forecast	advised	announced
disagreed	agreed	explained
maintained	argued	described
contradicted	introduced	emphasized
indicated	decided	assured

3 Peter Jordan has applied the eight techniques of formal written style that were presented in Chapter 7: he has avoided:
● personal pronouns
● contractions

- long sentences
- repetition

and he has used:

- passive voice structure
- impersonal 'it' constructions
- formal vocabulary
- clear linking techniques.

How would you report the following five statements?

1	*Andy*	'I'm sorry, I've forgotten the report but I'll let you have it on your desk first thing in the morning.'
2	*Jacques*	'You know we can't allow the welding job to be done in the gas plant without making sure safety procedures are followed.'
3	*Jane*	'What you are suggesting, John, is not acceptable to me.'
4	*Spencer*	'I'd already written the report when the circular came round.'
5	*Vinod*	'The control valve PV325 must be changed at once.'

If you want to project the SOLDIER image, then the three techniques used by Peter Jordan in his report on the highway development meeting ought to be applied to these sentences. Once you have written your version compare it with the following:

1 Andy promised that the report would be available early the following morning.

2 Jacques insisted that the welding work in the gas plant should not be conducted without proper safety precautions.

3 Jane disagreed with John's suggestion.

4 The report had already been written when the notice arrived.

5 Vinod ordered the immediate replacement of control valve PV325.

You will notice that these changes make the sentences very formal, precise and clear. To achieve this style will require plenty of practice. The important points, however, for producing effective recordings of discussions are:

- Take notes on decisions.
- Identify important information required by the reader to appreciate the decisions.
- Ensure all information is selected and labelled under separate sections.

- Labels (subheadings) in the formal recording of a discussion help to avoid wordiness.
- Write your first draft of the record of a meeting *immediately* following the meeting.

Summary

Letter writing and the recording of discussions are examples of documents that can easily occasion conflict. The sensitivity aspect therefore needs to be addressed in the production of documents which:

- will reflect the image projected by the company producing them, i.e. letters, and
- will attempt to summarize the precise expression of a speaker at a meeting, interview or during a telephone conversation.

Letters need to be more informal, personal and friendly in tone and style than documentation which is for in-company use, for although the communication may be between organization and organization, the correspondence is invariably between person and person.

When recording discussions, you will need to be precise and exact, logical and concise, but above all, sensitive to personal, cultural and political aspects of the people whose conversation you are recording.

11 Applying successful techniques

In this chapter you will first analyse an ineffective report and then, in a case study, you will be asked to report on a problem which will require an application of the four phases of the production process.

There is a tendency for people who produce reports to put pen to paper or fingers to word processors without really thinking or planning the project through. There is nothing disastrously wrong with this approach; many people prefer this method, claiming that they can think, plan and write simultaneously. The danger, of course, is that the document will not address the reader, will be difficult to absorb and ultimately become too wordy.

A more systematic approach would ensure that documents leaving your desk are fashioned in the image you want to project. If you want to project an image that is:

> Sensitive
> Organized
> Loyal
> Decisive
> Intelligent
> Efficient
> Responsible

then all these facets should be reflected in your reports.

An ineffective report

Case study

Consider Karl Friedmann's document. Would you say he has the competitive edge, the will to succeed, the dash of distinction? Or would you consider him muddled, disorganized and unsure?

Karl Friedmann is a project engineer working for Krestel AG, a company engaged in oil recovery. His major involvement is in developing project proposal formats and construction packages for a well-casing protection programme which will ultimately provide protection for more than 1300 well casings. He is also working in a supervisory capacity on the installation of cathodic protection systems for major hydrocarbon pipelines and is responsible for mobilization of contractors, manpower planning, contractor/client interface, site supervision and general contract administration.

Note: cathodic protection is an anti-corrosion technique for metal installations—pipelines, tanks, buildings—in which weak electric currents are set up to offset the current associated with metal corrosion. Carbon or non-ferrous anodes buried near the pipeline are connected to the pipe. Current flowing from the corroding anode to the metal installation controls the corrosion of the installation.

Here is Karl's report.

To: Project Manager   Date: 27 December 19__

From: Project Engineer Ref: P/412789

Subject: Annual Adjustive Survey for
          Consideration

(1)   In the past the cathodic protection annual adjustive
      survey has been conducted from within the
      department. As the area, together with the number of
      cathodic protection systems has increased,
      comprehensive surveys to determine the overall
      protective levels throughout the area, have and will
      take up more of the Inspectorate's time.

(2)   This is an inherent problem which appears to have
      manifested itself to gargantuan proportions,
      ultimately culminating in the present annual report
      which has taken virtually six months to complete.
      I feel that this is an unreasonable time span.
      I further feel that a format should be drawn up for
      surveys covering the complete survey method from
      leaving the office to returning with data. I have
      taken the liberty of outlining a number of things I
      feel could be considered by you and possibly
      observed by the Inspectorate to expedite the next
      annual survey in a more plausible period of time.

(3) Primarily, each inspector could prepare a programme together with a completion forecast of all structures in his area, broken down into categories (pipelines, major and minor, etc.) for submission to yourselves for evaluation and priority setting, all Inspectorate could begin surveys on the same type of structures thus achieving conformity. This conformity would enable one particular area, say processed daily and preferably typed to improve presentation. Data and the method of obtaining and recording could be standardized to avoid confusion at the interpretation stage. With the completion of a particular structure a brief synopsis of the survey would also help; for example, a description of the type of system, general condition of the rectifier together with tap settings and any other observations, rectifier meters should be checked also. The type of ground bed could be mentioned, its installation date and relevant performance. A topographical comment on the area of the structure could also be relevant to performance and might be worth including. An interpretation of the readings obtained together with the inspector's viewpoint for remedying an ailing system in some cases would help to identify problem areas and assist in conclusions and recommendations. With all the Inspectorate presenting uniform reports and data, as well as adopting the same survey procedures, I feel collation and compilation would be infinitely more simple and have a streamlining effect on the whole operation.

(4) The desired effect could make coordination, compilation and writing of the report a daily activity, as previously mentioned, potential data could be processed and typed daily as well. With more time becoming (hopefully) available at the writing stage I feel a more comprehensive style could be adopted thus giving a much clearer picture of structures and their respective systems' efficiency or deficiency as the case may be. I feel

we have tended to omit detail in an effort to get the reports out and therefore suggest the following format for your consideration.

(5) <u>Suggested Format for Survey</u>

a. Programme   to be prepared by inspector
                                and submitted

b. Completion Forecast   to be prepared by inspector
                                and engineer

c. Structure Breakdown   to be prepared by inspector

d. Priorities   to be determined by
                                engineer

e. Standardization of   to be determined by
   Survey Procedures   engineer

f. Standard Data Forms   to be prepared by engineer

g. Standard Method of   to be determined by
   Tabulation   engineer

h. Rectifier Data &   to be recorded by inspector
   Observations

i. System Description   to be recorded by inspector

j. System & Survey   to be submitted by
   Synopsis   inspector

k. Adjustive Measures   to be recorded by inspector
   Taken

<u>Suggested Format for Report</u>

a. Subject   )
)
b. Description   ) Introduction
)
c. History   )

d. Object   ) As One
e. Survey Method   )

f. Observations   )
)
g. Data Interpretation   )
)
h. Discussion   ) Itemized
)
i. Conclusion   )
)
j. Recommendation   )

k. Data   )
) Separate Section
l. Profiles   )

(6)   The word 'adjustive' as used in our survey heading
literally means 'to bring into a satisfactory state,
to rectify, to make more effective and conformable
in relation to a corresponding subject'. That would,
therefore, suggest we are adopting remedial tactics
as and when a problem area is encountered. I think
not, we are merely producing a list of potential
readings. Should a system be devalued due to
defective insulating flanges, we just report it as
is and issue worksheets. Should we not 'adjust' the
system in an effort to achieve protective levels
prior to repair of insulating flanges, and then
'readjust' or recommission the system when (if ever)
the maintenance crew effect repairs. As our reports
stand, we are in fact quite openly saying, 'this is
protected, this is not, we have not done anything
about it, but we have recorded the date, we know the
flanges will be replaced eventually, until then it
is not protected'!

(7)   This will, obviously, be a point of some discussion
as not all situations involving problem areas can be
attributed to flanges. This point, together with all
the foregoing points are purely suggestions made in
an effort to produce a more presentable and
professional document which will be more accurate,
factual and acceptable to the proponents who rely on

> its contents for guidance when assessing external
> corrosion problems.
>
> (8)   I trust some of the foregoing contents will prove of
> interest.

You may think that this report is an extraordinary document produced especially for the sake of pointing out weaknesses. It certainly is
not. In fact, it is typical. The writer has not planned his report; he has
not thought about his ultimate aim in producing his report; he has not
chosen his words with care and consideration.

The project engineer realizes that he has a problem with the annual
survey report. He has a solution that he must *sell* to his boss. He should
also realize that his recommendations require a certain amount of
explanation before being presented.

The paragraphs of Karl Friedmann's report have been numbered to
help you appreciate the following critique.

Information control

There is too much information content in paragraph 2 where Karl
over-explains the effects of the current procedure. In paragraph 3 he is
proposing a procedure: such a text should be listed and numbered. This
would allow the reader (and the writer!) to distinguish the wood from
the trees and avoid repetition. The effects of his proposal also need to be
listed and numbered in paragraph 4. This would preclude the needless
repetition of *I feel*. Furthermore, the explanation of the term 'adjustive'
should surely have been positive rather than the negative speech style
presented in paragraph 6. As for paragraph 7, it is not only redundant
but laughable. In conclusion, the final line of this persuasive report will
certainly not motivate the reader to action!

To be effective, this document would need to be radically edited to
present a suitable sequence of ideas. The writer should formulate an
appropriate subject heading, explain the present procedure, highlight
the problems it occasions, propose a remedy and finally emphasize the
positive effects of his proposal.

Language control

The repetition of the words *I feel* give the document a tentative tone
which does not support Karl's proposition. The text needs to be more
assertive and direct even though it is addressed to his superior.

What do you think about the changes in the following sentences? They are all taken from paragraph 2.

I feel that this is an unreasonable time span.
The time span seems rather unreasonable.

I further feel that a format should be drawn up for surveys covering the complete survey method.
A format could be drawn up which covers the complete survey method.

I have taken the liberty of outlining a number of things I feel could be considered by you and possibly observed by the Inspectorate to expedite the next annual survey in a more plausible period of time.
The following recommendations would assist in expediting the next annual survey.

The text is written in a rather informal style and is full of tentatively expressed opinions all beginning with *I*. This focuses the reader's attention on the author rather than on the writer's main area of concern.

The report makes infrequent use of sentences which begin with the issue under focus. When the writer does begin with such a subject we get an acceptable style, as in paragraph 2: *Data and the method of obtaining and recording it could be standardized to avoid confusion at the interpretation stage.*

Some of the words and phrases are too colloquial; others just do not make sense, e.g.

Paragraph 3	*Primarily ...*	superfluous
Paragraph 3	*might be worth including ...*	speech
Paragraph 6	*I think not ...*	speech
Paragraph 6	*As our reports stand ...*	speech
Paragraph 7	*a point of some discussion ...*	wrong word
Paragraph 7	*together with all the foregoing points ...*	superfluous
Paragraph 8		nonsense

Presentation techniques

Finally, on the third criterion of acceptability, the report fails lamentably—*it does not look attractive*. Subheadings and numbered points would help the reader to appreciate the information content; indentations, lists and tables would also help.

The project manager should be able to assimilate the contents of such a document in seconds. In its present format it would take several minutes.

A more acceptable version of this document follows. You may like to rewrite the report in the light of this analysis and then compare your efforts with the version below.

To: Project Manager   Date: 27.8.9_

From: Project Engineer   Ref: P/412789

Subject: Proposed Format on the Cathodic Protection
          Annual Survey and Report

In the past the cathodic protection annual adjustive survey has been conducted by the department. As both the area and number of cathodic protection systems have increased, surveys have consumed a larger part of the Inspectorate's time.

As a result, the present annual report has taken six months to complete. This is not a reasonable time span.

It is recommended therefore that each inspector should prepare a survey programme of all structures in his area. The survey should include the following:

— A brief description and general condition of the cathodic protection system.

— Topographical views in the vicinity of the studied structure.

To expedite the next annual survey, the attached formats covering the survey and reporting methods are suggested.

(1)

<u>Suggested Format for Survey</u>

<u>Action</u>	<u>Prepared by</u>
Programme	Inspector
Completion Forecast	Inspector and Engineer
Structure Breakdown	Inspector
Priorities	Engineer
Standardization of Survey Procedures	Engineer
Standard Data Forms	Engineer
Standard Method of Tabulation	Engineer
Rectifier Data and Observations	Inspector
System Description	Inspector
System and Survey Synopsis	Inspector
Adjustive Measures Taken	Inspector

(2)

Suggested Format for Report

1. Recommendations

2. Conclusions

3. Subject   )
)
4. Description   )   Introduction
)
5. History   )

6. Object   )
)   As one
7. Survey Method   )

8. Observations   )
)
9. Data Interpretation)   Itemized
)
10. Discussion   )

11. Data   )
)   Attachments
12. Profiles   )

                  (3)

The image factor is very important for any successful manager or supervisor and should always be given high priority when you are reviewing a final draft. Successful people are proud of their reports. The phrase *author's pride* has a poignant meaning.

If your documents pass the threefold test of information control, language control and presentation techniques then you will have produced a document that:

● can be understood at a first reading—CLEAR

- is expressed intelligently and intelligibly in a minimum number of words—CONCISE
- has the tone, style and presentation techniques applied throughout the entire paper—CONSISTENT
- includes sufficient and necessary information—COMPLETE
- will stand up to verification—CORRECT

Final case study

You are a senior executive officer working for Crown Chase Bancorporation (CCB), a multibank holding company based in Dallas, Texas, USA. You believe that CCB should expand its foreign operations by entering the European market to serve their prime corporate customers. These are multinational organizations whose own clients are busily modifying operations because of the Europhoria which has taken over from decades of Europessimism. On 1 July 19— a single market for financial services opened for business in eight European Community countries. Spain and Ireland are due to join in January of next year and Portugal and Greece will complete the picture two years later.

Thus, most Europeans can now open a bank account, make investments or take out a mortgage anywhere in Europe. Banks are now able to offer a wide range of services. This single financial area is both an opportunity and a challenge.

You feel that your only European branch, London, will not be able to serve the Continental market adequately. Therefore, you wish to capitalize on the buoyant industrial, commercial and financial developments in Europe by opening a CCB branch on the European mainland. You have not totally convinced your chief executive officer, Mal King, about your proposal but since he has the final decision you must convince him on paper that:

1 opening another European branch is essential, especially with current European developments;
2 CCB should have a representative office as an initial type of operation;
3 Marseilles, and not Brussels, Paris or Milan, should be the location.

Last year, as you were not totally convinced of the viability of this project yourself, you commissioned four specialists working at CCB headquarters in Dallas to study various aspects of this venture and report back to you. These reports form the main supporting arguments for your proposal.

The Askin Report focuses on projected operating costs for a full branch in Brussels, Paris, Marseilles and Milan.

The Brady Report is a review of Askin's initial study and makes projections for five years for each of the four locations.

The Croft Report deals with the potential risks and returns of various options of the proposed expansion. These were:

- a joint venture
- full branch
- representative office
- buy into a European bank

The Duncan Report covers the legal aspects of opening a branch within the new European Constitution.

You have just completed a study of all the reports and can now prepare your proposal. Details and supportive data will be in the four in-depth studies described above, which will be attachments. You first scribble some notes: these you will use to support your proposal.

Marseilles is the capital of Bouche-du-Rhône department and the second largest city in France. It is located on the Côte d'Azur just west of the French Riviera. Business people can relax in an environment of serene tranquillity, thus relieving the stress and pressure of international transactions.

Marseilles is also a major manufacturing centre. Petroleum refining, ship building and steel are the chief industries.

In comparison with the other locations it is a relatively underbanked city. There is only one other American bank in Marseilles, while there are as many as ten in Paris, five in Brussels and three in Milan.

As a seaport it has quick and easy access to many of the other countries in the EC: Spain, Italy, Greece and Portugal.

The expected returns are higher than any of the other three locations.

In terms of profitability and costs, the proposal makes economic sense. Although a full branch would eventually be more profitable than a representative office, it is more risky and more costly.

The control factor is a very strong argument supporting the proposal. The full branch would demand independent control; the joint venture could mean hours of wrangling in the conference room. The French and the English tend to mix like oil and water, and 'the English' means the English-speaking, not just the British. The same argument quashes the option of buying *into* a French bank.

The legal constraints of establishing a representative office in France are minimal. Therefore in terms of risks and constraints, the representative office is of low risk because any losses would be small relative to the potential return.

As a senior executive officer for CCB you will have to go through the process of:

- thinking
- planning
- writing, then
- revising

if an effective document is going to be produced, reflecting the image you wish to project.

To help yourself in the thinking stage consider:

1 To whom are you writing?
2 What is the *reader's* chief interest with regard to this report?
3 How will he use the supportive information?
4 How will he benefit from reading this report?
5 If this were an oral report what questions do you think he might ask on completion of your presentation?
6 What problems do you anticipate on the grounds of:
   - diplomacy
   - company policy
   - resistance to change
   - scepticism?
7 Will your reader appreciate an argument from or to the principal aim?
8 When he has finished reading the report what do you want him *to do*?
9 To achieve this objective, how will you need to marshall your written thoughts?
10 Are there any aspects with regard to your aim with this report, for this reader, that may not have been considered? *Think*!

NOTE: These ten considerations can apply to any writing project you may have.

From the information you have, **plan** your topic outline. Once you have your outline, compare it with the one given in the next chapter. You can then write your report either from your own topic outline, or the one given, then compare it with the version offered in the next chapter.

12 Revising for the precise impact

Once you have written your document and are satisfied with your efforts it is advisable—especially with a long and important project—to put it aside for a day. Then, when you give it that final review in your search for the image you wish to project, you will be fresh and alert.

When you are revising a document, be critical with respect to:
- the language
- the structure
- the 'feel' of the message

To assess the 'feel' of the message, ask yourself: *Will this document have exactly the impact I wish to make?* Small adjustments may be necessary to words, structure or grammar.

Revision checklists

To help you check the language aspects ask yourself:

1 Are some sentences too long?
2 Does the text flow naturally?
3 Are there any unnecessary words or phrases?
4 Are all sentences expressed clearly and without ambiguity?
5 Could a sentence be changed and made more effective by 'fronting' the focal issue or vice versa?
6 Is there a sentence containing too much information?
7 Can pronouns be identified immediately and without reader effort?
8 Has jargon been avoided? Have I used words my reader can understand?
9 Can any ideas be expressed more formally by changing a word or phrase?
10 Is the text grammatically correct?

Now evaluate the report and make sure you can tick all the 'yes' boxes.

	Yes	*No*
1 Does the report look attractive?	[Y]	[N]
2 Is the information necessary/sufficient?	[Y]	[N]
3 Does the subject heading relate to the central issue and minimize reader guesswork?	[Y]	[N]
4 Is it possible to identify different parts of the document easily and quickly?	[Y]	[N]
5 Have you used diagrams, charts and tables when and where necessary?	[Y]	[N]
6 Can the reader follow the logical sequence of your ideas?	[Y]	[N]
7 Is the tone appropriate?	[Y]	[N]
8 Have you avoided spoken patterns where possible?	[Y]	[N]
9 Have you eradicated all possible ambiguities?	[Y]	[N]
10 Are you proud of your document?	[Y]	[N]

Now, as a practical exercise, apply both these sets of guidelines to the final report you planned and wrote as an exercise in the preceding chapter. A model version of the report follows the topic outline.

Topic outline

Introduction

1.0 Single European Market

1.1 European Developments
1.2 Customer Needs

2.0 Location

2.1 Major Options
2.2 Marseilles
    2.2.1 Area Capital
    2.2.2 Environment
    2.2.3 Industries
    2.2.4 Competition
    2.2.5 Seaport Facilities
    2.2.6 Operating Costs

3.0 Functional Options

3.1 Buy into a French Bank
3.2 Joint Venture
3.3 Full Branch
3.4 Representative Office
3.5 Legal Implications
3.6 Risks/Returns

4.0 Returns on Investment

5.0 Profitability and Costs

6.0 Recommendations

Model report

To:	Mal King, CEO	*Date:*	26 February 19__
From:	N. J. Butler, SEO	*Ref:*	287/AXB
Subject:	**Proposed Expansion of Crown Chase Bancorporation into Europe**		

1.0 Single European Market

1.1 European Developments

From July 1, 19__ a single market for financial services opens for business in eight European Community countries. Furthermore, two years later, Spain and Ireland will follow. After another two years Portugal and Greece will also join the market.

1.2 Customer Needs

Most Europeans today can open a bank account, make investments or take out a mortgage anywhere in Europe. A wide range of services are offered by most banks.
For Crown Chase Bancorporation the single European market represents a challenge, as well as an opportunity, to capitalize on the buoyant industrial, commercial and financial developments of the area.

2.0 Location

  2.1 Major Options

    It is felt that our only existing European branch, London, is not able to provide an adequate service to the single market. Brussels, Paris and Milan would not be suitable locations for expansion for the reasons listed in the appended reports.

  2.2 Marseilles

    2.2.1 Area Capital

      Not only is Marseilles the capital of Bouche-du-Rhône, it is the second largest city in France.

    2.2.2 Environment

      Located on the Côte d'Azur it attracts many businesses with European, North African and Middle Eastern concerns.

    2.2.3 Industries

      Chief industries of this major manufacturing city include petroleum refining, ship building and steel.

    2.2.4 Competition

      With only one other American bank, compared with ten in Paris, five in Brussels and three in Milan, Marseilles is relatively underbanked.

    2.2.5 Seaport Facilities

      Easy access is afforded to many of the other countries in the EC.

    2.2.6 Operating Costs

      The Askin Report in Appendix A deals adequately with this consideration.

3.0 Available Options

  3.1 Buying into a French Bank

    This is not considered to be a viable option because of the current attitude of France to Anglo–American business.

  3.2 Joint Venture

    Although a future attraction, at present this option could mean hours of wrangling in the conference room without ever reaching a mutual agreement.

  3.3 Full Branch

    Independent control would be demanded, resulting in loss of control by the holding company in Dallas, if this were allowed.

3.4 Representative Office

As an initial type of operation, this is to be preferred because of the minimal legal constraints and low potential return.

3.5 Legal Implications

The Duncan Report in Appendix D covers the legal aspects pertaining to the new European constitution and would support the representative office proposal.

3.6 Risks and Returns

In Appendix C the Croft Report deals with potential risks and returns of the various options. The idea of a representative office once again is favourable.

4.0 Returns on Investment

Marseilles is expected to generate the highest returns of the locations examined.

5.0 Profitability and Costs

5.1 Full Branch

Eventually this option could prove the most profitable but it is currently too risky and costly.

5.2 Representative Office

This is a less profitable, but less risky and less costly option, and is therefore recommended.

6.0 Recommendations

6.1 It is expected that Marseilles will produce higher returns than Brussels, Milan or Paris.

6.2 Marseilles has more advantages over the other locations, especially if a representative office is considered as an initial venture.

Index